Waiting

for the

Fruit to Ripen

One Adoptive Family's Experiences While Beginning to
Heal the Invisible Wounds of RAD and PTSD

Mary Ray

With Gratitude and Dedication:

Mama, K. C., and K. H.

Without your support, this story would not have been written.

Thanks for your knowledge, encouragement, commitment, and love.

Waiting For the Fruit to Ripen

Adopting a child is an amazing thing. Adopting two is simply incredible. Realizing that the children you so desperately want to love cannot accept that love- that leaves you speechless. The amazingly difficult, incredibly depressing task that comes with adopting children from traumatic backgrounds is one that words can't describe. This book tells the story of one family's struggles and triumphs as they embark on the journey to healing.

This family was formed by the adoption of brothers, ages 3 and 6. With tremendous support, healing has begun for the children and their mother. The first two years were full of confusing, hurtful, and difficult times. Along with the boys' challenging behaviors, the legal, financial, and emotional stressors were overwhelming.

All adoptive families are likely to have stories of their own. Many families with children from traumatic backgrounds might relate to the anecdotes detailed. This story does not end with disruption, and it is likely that many other families have had to endure more significant disturbances than these children exhibited. The message is:

In many adoptive families, struggles are common. With support, it was possible for this family to pull through the rough times during the first two years together. Mistakes were made during this difficult period, but progress still emerged. The circumstances, while seemingly unfortunate to begin with, proved to be beneficial as time went on. Not all families are as lucky. The children, while difficult, had the protective factor of youth, and the parent had the support of her mother and an amazing, competent, and all-knowing therapist. Two years is a long time, but not long enough to heal the deeply wounded heart. While this story ends on a positive note, the healing continues into the future.

The names have been changed in this story, but everything else is absolutely true. My friend and I have an ongoing joke that if either of us were ever to write a book, it would have to be sold as fiction. I'll just have to see how this goes. Please enjoy our story, and if you are a parent of a child who has similarities to the ones described in this book, please know that you are not alone. That bit of knowledge helped me more than anyone can know.

Reactive Attachment Disorder (RAD), as I've read, is common among adopted children, as well as those with disrupted attachments due to parental stress, vision problems, health problems, or other issues that prevent bonding. The attachment might be disrupted or nonexistent. In my sons' cases, I believe that my oldest son had attachment, but it was disrupted, and my youngest never developed attachment to a caregiver. Both of them struggle with relationships, but my oldest initially displayed symptoms that are much more obvious. My oldest son, when I began reading up on the disorder, exhibited almost every marker for RAD. He is nowhere near healed, but is now showing some signs of attachment.

Post-Traumatic Stress Disorder (PTSD) is another common diagnosis among adopted children, especially those adopted at an older age. My children were 3 and 6 years old when I adopted them, and had witnessed things I cannot imagine. Some things, I still don't know, and likely never will. Certain reactions give me clues, like when my son becomes very stressed as he watches something that shows the possibility of injury for anyone or anything. Any reference to affection or love also causes devastation. Both of my sons react severely to people they perceive to have physical similarities to their former grandmother and grandfather. Locations where experiences with those people have taken place are also "trauma triggers", and cause serious anxiety. My children react significantly even at the mention of those people or places.

Love (LOVE) is hard. Love is impossible for my children, even as I write this book. My youngest son is beginning to feel it, and my oldest is approaching it. Love alone cannot heal these kids, but without it, nothing will change. I had no problem loving my kids, but I can see that without our therapist, my mom, and my background and knowledge in child development, I would not have survived all of what my sons dealt me. They were nearly impossible. They were cute, little, and apparently sweet, though. Everyone else saw them that way. I did, too, until things changed when they came to realize that I was here to stay. That was what did it. Anyone willing to love them had to be destroyed. They tried to make that happen. They wanted me to give up on them. Then everything they'd ever known would have been confirmed. They were nothing. That was not true, but they believed it. The screaming in the car, the fits, the refusal to eat, the oppositional behavior, the failure to respect boundaries. All of these behaviors played a role in our struggle, but we survived- to this point, at least. I can't pretend to know your situation, but I know this:

Life is hard, and my kids made it even harder. I hope, with every ounce of my being, that everyone who understands this story has the courage to go on and try to heal their child. The other thing I hope for is that these kids can actually be healed. I get through each day with that hopeful thought.

Many families are formed through the adoption of children who have experienced trauma. I can't assume that all families go through the same kind of struggle as our family did. What I can say, with absolute certainty, is that my family has endured great difficulty. We continue to press forward, working to heal the invisible wounds. The journey will never end, but we now walk through life together. My boys are the joy of my life, and I have no regrets in my decision to adopt. In the beginning, I could never have used "unripened" as a way to describe them. They were bitter and sour, but the concept of ripening wasn't there. Rotten was more like it. They had an overly sweet appearance, but the good inside was difficult to find. I am forever grateful that I could somehow keep strong enough to experience the true sweetness that is a part of them. It simply needed time and support to develop.

Before reading, please understand that I am not an expert in Reactive Attachment Disorder, or Post Traumatic Stress Disorder. I am simply learning through my experiences as I parent two children with those problems. Our family has gone through a lot. Some of the issues, like the stress from legal and financial struggles do not necessarily directly relate to the RAD and PTSD anyway. What is important to realize, however, is that stress within a family is significant, and when children with special needs are involved, *any* stress is potentially overwhelming.

The strong feelings and mistakes made are described without sugar-coating. It's real. I'm ashamed about that. I don't like the way I behaved, but I realize that I cannot change what happened. I can only work harder in the future, continue to learn about my children, and find better ways to effectively deal with their behaviors and my stress. I still get hurt, but can cope much better than I once could. I now realize that no matter how hard things are for me, my children are suffering more. I have to be strong for them. I don't always do as well as I feel I should, but there is no lack of effort. Someday, we'll all be much better. In the meantime, I must be strong and consistent in my actions. I hope that my honesty can help other families to feel less isolated in their struggles. I am still working to help my children "ripen" fully, but am holding on to the hope that someday, sweetness will come to stay.

Before They Were Mine

Before they (my beautiful boys) were mine, I knew their birthmother. She was younger than I, a neighbor. My sister babysat her as a child. Proximity and circumstance kept us in contact- she was briefly employed at my workplace as an adult, even. Her parents were always frightening to me, but I can't explain why. The mother, with a slight build and pockmarked face, didn't present herself as a person with the ability to win a fight. Her glaring eyes and hesitating speech could make me uneasy, however. She had a kind of half-smile, and would move her mouth as if trying to find her words just before she voiced a carefully planned insult. This, to me, was hard to read. It was an odd way of communicating. She would stare and remain silent as if the words spoken to her were so ridiculous that she couldn't even justify them with a response. Then, just as she seemed to find her words, the awkward smile would break through, and her disdainful tone could be heard. The father (former grandfather to my children), a large man, concealed his face with a beard and mustache. His dry voice and yellowed teeth showed the results of years of smoking. The birthmother also had a half-sister about my age that was sent away at about 12 after accusing her stepfather of sexually abusing her. I suspect that she spoke the truth about the abuse, and am concerned because my sons spent time in the "care" of an accused molester.

The boys' birthmother became pregnant in high school, and had my oldest son, James, prior to graduating. She seemed to take good care of him for his first year. He was well-fed, clean, and seemed happy. He likely witnessed domestic altercations, but showed no signs of abnormality. The birthmother attempted to live life as a family with the birthfather, and stayed with him, despite his frequent arrests due to drug charges. They had Jackson, my youngest son, a few years later but the situation at the time of his birth was not nearly as positive. The police were frequently involved due to domestic violence and drugs. The birthfather was incarcerated at the time of Jackson's birth. The birthmother admittedly used drugs and smoked, even voicing the desire for a "small baby". Jackson was born slightly early and had complications that required him to be transferred to a facility in a larger town that was capable of treating premature newborns. He seemed to recover fully, and thankfully shows no signs of developmental delays related to his birth. At about that time, the birthmother became diagnosed with Crohn's disease, and required major surgery for an impacted bowel. The drugs she was given for the physical pain provided her with a way to suppress the emotional pain, as well. She became addicted to drugs and her boyfriend was very capable of supplying her with them. Drugs became more important than anything to her. She ended up leaving the boys at her parents' house, although they did not allow her to stay there. At the time, both her mother and father lived there together, though not peacefully. The two of them soon separated, and the former grandfather left the home to live in their camper. Within a week, he was told by the former grandmother to come get the children, or she would turn them over to the state. My boys were very clearly told that nobody wanted them. They still refer to that particular move from the

6

house to the camper as "being kicked out". They spent about a year with their former grandfather in the camper. James began kindergarten while living there. He spent most of his time in trouble at school, and was even suspended for his behavior. Both boys were wearing inappropriate clothing. The clothes were too small, unsuitable for the season, and dirty. The former grandmother would occasionally (once every few weeks or so, for a while) take James to church with her. She would dress him in nice clothing that had been donated to the birthmother by a friend from work, and then have him change back into his other clothes before going back to the camper. From what I've been told, there were constant arguments, fighting, yelling, and physical altercations in front of the boys. Police reports were made, and protection orders filed, but nobody ever followed through with them, aside from one domestic battery case against the former grandfather, for which he was granted a diversion. Child abuse and neglect were reported, but nothing came of it, either. During this time, the boys saw little of their birthmother, and after she had stolen her parents' credit cards, they pressed charges against her on Christmas Day. Her mother went to her sentencing hearing and pleaded with the judge to lock her up for as long as possible, and that's what happened. She had no contact with the boys or her parents until I began talking with her about guardianship for the boys.

James, at 6, was a bit small for his age, but not so much that it was really noticeable. His toothy smile was displayed more times than not. He would have an open-mouth grin, even as he was sitting in a chair while in trouble at school. Jackson, 3, did not seem to have the ability to smile. His round little cheeks were still, with emotion held in. He would stand with his fists clenched, but his face remained emotionless. His mouth typically stayed closed, and his big brown eyes were sad. He appeared distant. Both boys were given their brown hair and eyes from their birthfather alone, but the hidden wounds had been given to them from all those involved.

Their birthmother, heavyset as a child, had lost a lot of weight as a young adult. Her teeth were lost as a result of drug use. She put a lot of weight back on, and would be provided with false teeth while incarcerated. Her blonde hair and blue eyes were not passed on to my sons, as the birthfather's dark hair and eyes from his own Hispanic father would remain dominant. The boys were cute, but in all honesty, it was not initially visible. Jackson couldn't give the ornery grin he has today- he was silent and solemn. James took on so much silliness that his smile, while large, was forced. I wouldn't get to see his real smile, dimples and all, for well over a year after we'd been together. His dark eyes were mysterious. Their long eyelashes (especially Jackson's) brought attention to those beautiful brown eyes, but I wouldn't come to learn about the fears, anger, and sadness hidden within them for quite some time. I had been a small part of their lives, but didn't really know them. I loved them, I suppose, as you love your unborn child. There is no explanation. Before I knew them as my sons, I loved them. Maybe it really was always meant to be. There is much debate on the unique connection between a mother and child, but I sincerely believe that blood has little to do with it.

The boys were treated differently within their first family. Although both boys were abused and neglected, James seemed to be the "chosen one" and was favored. He had been given birthday parties every year, while Jackson never had one. James was the one to be brought with "Nana", while Jackson was not. Jackson was not to touch anything that "belonged" to James. Jackson experienced life as a "second-rate" person, and James, although similarly abused, came to the conclusion that the worth of a person could be measured, and he had an edge over Jackson. James was 6, and appeared overly silly, but was somewhat compliant. Jackson was 3, displayed little positive emotion, and was more or less just the shell of a child. He was just "there". He went along for the ride, and occasionally expressed his discontent, but never his pleasure.

As for me, I had been looking into adoption even before the boys were a possibility. I had been engaged, but broke it off before getting into a marriage that lacked a good relationship. I am very dedicated to my work, and am not overly social. The image I had of a family with a loving husband and children by birth was not looking like it would become a reality. I was planning to wait until I was completely financially secure before I began seriously looking into the adoption process. I looked at the pictures and stories of children waiting for families, and figured that one day I would go ahead and do it. I was waiting to afford to buy a house rather than rent, and to have some money put away.

I am a teacher, and I work at my mom's early childhood center. My sister also works for the program. I teach preschool during the school year, and work with school-age children after school and during the summer. James ended up coming to be at my building after school for a short time every day during his kindergarten year. It was during this time that I voiced my wish to a coworker that those boys would be the ones I could adopt. I never imagined that it would ever really happen. You don't just go and say- "Hey, those kids need a better life, I am just going to be their mom instead." Although it seems that it happened almost like that, I don't feel that it's right for people to pretend that they should just take over if they think they can be a better parent. It is hard to believe that it happened the way it did- even though I lived it!

Before they were mine, I spent almost all my time at work, home, or caring for my very dear elderly friend. I was pretty happy, pretty good at my job, and didn't have any debt other than a car loan. I was patient most of the time, secure in who I was, and generally content. I realized that my life would change when I adopted children, but the magnitude of the events to come was not something I could have ever dreamed of.

On the surface, the actions I took during the process of becoming a family seem cold, I think. Although I am not necessarily comfortable with the decisions I made along the way, the confusion and overwhelming uncertainty made things challenging. The legal battles and misunderstandings caused great difficulty. I will be very happy if I never again have to deal with courts (or crazy people) again.

The Messy Beginning

I had looked at my boys, wishing they were mine for a long time. I knew the situation, but couldn't imagine approaching their birthmother, incarcerated, to obtain guardianship of the boys. She hadn't been taking care of them even before she was in prison. I felt that they deserved better. I wanted them to have a good life, but I felt that it was not my place to go and try to take over their care. Their former grandparents were supposed to be responsible for them. The state's investigations of abuse and neglect were ruled unfounded. Who was I to say that just because I thought I could do better for them, I had the right to barge in and take over? It was just a thought- not a realistic expectation. I was still spending my time looking at those pictures of children waiting for adoption through our state agency. Those were the kids I expected to eventually adopt. Then, in the middle of a busy summer, the craziness began. I believe that things happened the way they did for a reason, but even now it is hard to take it all in. Maybe, just maybe, the excessive insanity of my sons' former grandparents actually worked in the boys' favor for once. The crazy former grandmother approached my family (intending for my sister to be the one to respond) about the boys being in danger. This woman -the same one who had made the statement that someone better come get the boys or she would give them to the state- gave a believable story about the former grandfather putting them in grave danger. I believe they were being harmed, but not any more than when she had also been responsible for their care. She did not have anything good to say about her husband. There was an incident involving a (certifiably) insane friend of his that took Jackson in the middle of the night to the former grandmother's house while James was staying there. The driver had Jackson in the front of the car, not restrained in a car seat, at the former grandmother's home. She believed that she was Superman, and felt that James needed a Superman toy while sleeping, in the middle of the night, at the former grandmother's home. This incident was described to me by the former grandmother, former grandfather, and by Jackson himself. He remembered the police, mostly. Even though this event is significant, I fully believe that the reasons behind the former grandmother's decision to approach us had little, if anything, to do with the boys' well-being. She was in the process of divorcing her husband, and since he had the boys in his care, he had a better chance at getting the house in the divorce. She was living alone in a 5 bedroom home, and he was living with the boys in a camper. It was a valid argument for him to get the house. In my opinion, she only wanted the boys out of the picture to prevent her husband from using them as leverage for the house in the divorce settlement. She still didn't want them. She outright admitted that she didn't. She gave various reasons, depending on her audience and current state of mind. Sometimes it was money, sometimes it was her health, other times it was their behavior. Regardless of the story she gave, she pretended to be overcome with emotion and cry every time she told one. Even after the joyride with Superman, she *still* didn't take the boys into her home. She didn't want them, she just didn't want her husband to have them. I wish I had been able to have such a cynical, yet realistic view at that point in time. I gave the crazy woman way too much benefit of doubt. I thought that maybe she did have too much financial stress, maybe she did have too many medical problems, maybe she wasn't as crazy as I thought she might be. I allowed her to use me in her ploy for control of everything. What she wasn't counting on was the fact that I truly cared for the boys- even before they were mine. I wanted what was best for them. I didn't trust her, but I didn't yet realize how awful she was. She really wanted my sister to be the one to care for the boys. I offered, but she kept talking as if my sister would be the one to do it. She must have come to realize that unless she relented in her notion that my sister would be the primary guardian, her ploy to have the boys away from her husband wouldn't work. My sister had a longer relationship with the family, as she had been the babysitter for the boys' birthmother for many years. The former grandfather was always looking for someone to take the boys for the weekend, and I offered to take them over the 4th of July, just two weeks before the guardianship would be approved. I kept the boys for the long weekend, and they did all right as far as behavior. I only remember going back to the car from a store once when I couldn't convince Jackson to get into the cart. He was 3 at the time, and has only tried that once since. They didn't want to go back with the former grandfather when the weekend was over, and I wanted so badly to tell them that I would be taking care of them soon. I couldn't tell them what I intended to do for many reasons. One reason was because at the time, I was unknowingly being manipulated into a devious scheme by their former grandmother. It was very wrong of me to go along with things as I did. I honestly can't figure out how I could have avoided it, given my lack of understanding at the time. I really wish I had been smarter about it, though.

I got in contact with the boys' birthmother, and she was more than willing to assist in giving me guardianship rights. She hadn't heard from her parents or kids at all since she'd been incarcerated.

My sister and I met with a lawyer, got papers drawn up, and filed for guardianship. At that time, guardianship was the only expectation. Adoption was mentioned briefly, but the attorney said that guardianship was basically the same thing. He said that the birthmother had to go to court to have the guardianship returned to her as it was. My only hard discussion with the birthmother was about my relationship with the boys in the future. I could not see myself caring for these boys and then suddenly giving them up. She was fine with the fact that I would remain a part of their lives. The agreement was that she would be their mother, but I would be the caregiver, even after her release. So we did it. My sister and I were given joint guardianship, and the boys were to live with me. I knew I hadn't gotten a down payment together for a house, and did not want to have the boys in an affordable apartment temporarily, only have to move again, so my poor parents became another part of this complicated matter. I wanted something safe, stable, and established for the boys. I later realized that the security of having other adults present would prove beneficial, as well. I didn't know then that finances were never going to be stable anyway. The costs ended up being so much higher than what we'd expected, substantial debt would contribute to our stressful existence. My parents were very helpful with every aspect of the situation, and honestly gave me no guilt or shame in my bringing two little boys into their home. My dad was a bit hesitant, but never showed my boys anything but what a good Grandpa was. I know it wasn't what he would have signed up for, but he was amazing, even with the difficulty it caused. My mom was amazingly, incredibly, indescribably supportive, as well. She was welcoming and helpful, and probably did more to help my dad come around than anything else. She kept everything going- laundry and food, and later on, kept me sane when things got rough. She naturally became the Grandma they needed.

14

So... the process began. I got the boys in a way that seems a little shady to me now. I can't entirely blame the crazy former grandmother (although I'd like to) for how things ended up playing out, because I should have been smarter. She gave us the impression that this had to be done secretively, so her husband couldn't just get something done to acquire guardianship himself (he only had power of attorney). She would not reach out to her daughter, even though she claimed she had, and would continue to lie about communicating with her. Someone had told her husband that he was about to lose the boys- I still don't know whether it was the birthmother or the former grandmother- both were capable of being deceitful. He had already petitioned for guardianship- one day prior to our papers being filed. The judge did not catch the error, and granted ours, too. When the former grandfather came to pick the boys up from daycare, ignorant of the fact that we, too, had filed for guardianship –this is the shady part- he was provided with the order for guardianship instead. I had gotten the boys already. Even taking into consideration the fact that I was misled, I have guilt about the way it happened. The boys knew me, and had stayed with me before, but it was rather abrupt. The former grandfather may be a poorly qualified caregiver- I'm pretty sure he is- but I am also sure that it was really difficult for things to happen the way they did. Even if he didn't really want to care for them, their sudden absence had to be hard to adjust to. As for the boys, they didn't want to go back with him, but it had to be hard for them to have their whole lives changed so significantly in a single day. I explained to them what was going on as well as I could. I told them that I thought that they needed better care than they were being given, and that I was going to take care of them for their "Mommy" instead of their former grandfather. James seemed to understand, but he states now that he didn't. He recently confided during therapy that he thought I might just throw him in the street to get run over or something. Jackson did not understand at all, for sure.

So, I got the boys. The papers were signed. I was now responsible for the care and well-being of two little boys. They went very willingly with me. There wasn't even a hint of hesitation. The ease of the transition troubled me, but I had nothing to compare their reaction to. I had no idea what a "normal" response should have been.

Our Lives Begin

That first day, I took them to a nearby town (honestly I was scared of the former grandfather hunting us down) to buy the essentials- toothbrushes, toothpaste, pajamas, underwear, socks, clothing, and a stuffed animal. I remember the first store we went to that evening. We picked up pajamas and clothing items, and headed to find the stuffed animals. I considered a stuffed animal to be a necessity. The selection was rather limited, and I really was intending to find cute teddy bears. The only soft animals that were not scary looking were some sock monkeys that came in a variety of colors. The event of choosing the monkeys was more significant than I ever could have imagined. I should have realized right then and there that James had an incredible ability to manipulate others. I noticed, but didn't think that it was important at the time. He picked his color for the monkey, and of course, little brother Jackson wanted the same. I encouraged a different color, so they would be able to tell them apart, and because James was incredibly displeased at the thought of allowing Jackson to have the same color. Jackson wasn't budging on the idea of having his blue monkey- the color James had chosen. The volcano was erupting, and Jackson was beginning to explode with a screaming fit. The siren wail that would soon become constant in our lives was increasing in volume with every second. I was stressed, and desperate to keep things calm. He began screaming "I want the blue one, I want the blue one!" My oldest son looked around, slyly put on a fake pitiful face and said with the saddest voice he could muster, "I guess I'll just have the yellow one". There was only one yellow monkey. Jackson took the blue monkey and hugged it tightly, but then realized he'd been had. He was stubborn enough not to say a word, though. He glanced up at the monkeys, and saw that there were no other yellow monkeys, while the echo from "I want the blue one!" was still ringing. He took the blue monkey, and James got the yellow one. I looked at James in awe. I said "I know what you did." He just grinned at me, very satisfied with himself. It wasn't even his silly, open-mouth grin. He was smiling with a sense of confidence and superiority. Jackson sat in the cart, still sniffling, holding the blue monkey. We went to a few more stores to pick up all we needed before heading home. It wasn't the most pleasant experience ever, but compared to the shopping trips I would take with them in the future, it ranks low on the scale of difficulty. They were not used to shopping, quite obviously, and wanted everything.

They suckered me into buying them new sunglasses, and were overwhelmed when I allowed them to choose their own toothbrushes. It became a 15 minute ordeal. Somehow, we made it through the shopping endeavor, and started for home. As we were driving back, I was either talking to myself, or answering a question from one of the boys about our destination. I said "We're going home now", and Jackson burst into tears. He began yelling "No!" and screaming- not the ear piercing scream I would soon come to know, but cries that expressed his displeasure very clearly. Anger and sadness were all pouring out at once, and I was confused. That's when James said these words "Not to Papa's. We're going to our new home." Jackson, upon hearing confirmation from me as I agreed with what James had told him, allowed himself to settle his violent cries into gentle sobs. He was ok with going "home", so long as it wasn't where he'd been staying before. I couldn't believe the reaction, honestly. We hadn't even had a lot of fun or done anything enjoyable. They had to be hungry, because we were planning to eat at home (oddly enough, the meal, beef and noodles, would be the one Jackson would later consider his favorite supper). There was plenty of crying and disappointment. Jackson had had little fits through most of the stores. He was mad that I was buying pull-ups. He was upset at the toothbrush he ended up with because it was not the same as the one James was getting. Everything was just all wrong. The only "toys" bought were the sock monkeys (monkeys, too, became Jackson's favorite animal), and the only indulgences were the pairs of sunglasses. The bulk of our purchases were basic necessities. It was not like I had gone on a spoil-the-kids-rotten shopping spree to try and buy their affection or desire to stay with me. We arrived home, ate, and I settled them into bed. I had left a phone number for the former grandfather to call to say good-night, but he did not call. I offered the boys the opportunity to call, but they declined.

Mixed Messages

The former grandmother implied that she was extremely close with the boys, and needed to say good night to them every night. I obliged, and provided the phone number for her, too. She called the first night. Only the first night. Then the undeniable evidence of insanity started to build. Quickly. Even though she didn't take the time to call to say "good night" to the boys, she suddenly wanted them to herself, on her terms. I don't like to seem overly negative, but given the experiences I'd had with this woman, I feel pretty confident stating that the reason for her sudden interest had little to do with the boys. I think that she wanted to be able to tell the former grandfather that she got to be around the boys and he couldn't. A display of control and power. The boys were not pleased when driving near her home *or* the camper's location. Jackson would scream inconsolably. It was evident that he did not want to be near either of them. A few days after they'd been with me, I ran out of clean pajamas for them, but grabbed a pair of shorts and a T-shirt for James. I didn't think it would be a problem, but it was. That was the first time I saw "the face" from James. He basically turned into an animal. I dislike referring to my son in that way, but his reaction can only be compared to that of a cornered animal. He gave a growl, opened up his mouth to let out an angry scream-like sound, and then returned to the moaning, growling sound. He pushed the shirt off of the bed. I am so glad that he did, because if he hadn't, I would never have made the connection that he was upset about the shirt. I had washed the shirt he came to me in, and it was the one I grabbed for him to sleep in. I never thought that he might have a problem wearing it. I asked him if he wanted to wear a plain T-shirt instead. I had one, but it was still in a shopping bag. He had backed himself into a corner, and was holding his arms up as if to protect himself from me coming at him. He didn't even seem to hear me at first. In fact, I'm not sure he ever heard me at all. I frantically looked for the new shirt, and I think he finally realized what I had been saying once I yanked the tags off of it. He then kind of acted like a baby. He grabbed the shirt, made some sounds- but no words, and started acting silly. I had no idea that he would even pay attention to the clothes I put out. I couldn't believe it. It made me wonder what possibly could have happened to him. Why would a T-shirt send him into such an odd state? I removed the shirt from the room, and told myself I would make sure that he never had to see it again. I was reassured that the abrupt transition was better than the alternative. I was just wishing that I had taken steps to get the boys sooner.

Jackson had issues with clothing, too, but not for the same reasons. The clothes he came in were so small (he was 3 years old, and the clothing was sized 24 months and 18 months) that I wouldn't have attempted to have him wear them again. His problems were mostly because he insisted on his clothing being similar to whatever James was wearing. He didn't care if it was identical, but if James had jean shorts, Jackson refused to dress unless he had jean shorts, too. The fabric type had to be the same for the shirt, too. He also had to be talked into wearing a pull-up at night. He never had an accident during the day, but he wet every night. He had been told that they didn't make pull-ups that

21

big. Only babies wet the bed. He did not like to be wet, but he did not want to be a baby. Once he realized that it wasn't a big deal, he really didn't fight it too much, although occasional fits over putting a pull-up on at night would persist for many months.

The biggest hurdle for Jackson was allowing me to touch him. He refused to be touched in any way. Picking him up- even just to put him in the car- was difficult. He was stiff as a board. His body did not adjust to being picked up. The second day I had the boys, we went to a program for my nieces and nephew. The space was limited, and the boys needed to sit on laps because there weren't enough seats. James, very wiggly, sat on my lap, and Jackson sat on my mom's lap, right next to me. He sat so far to the edge of her legs that he must have only had a half an inch of his body on her knees. She instinctively put her hands on him to keep him from falling off of her lap. He took her hands and removed them from him. It was pitiful. He could not stand to be touched. This was a huge hurdle to overcome. It was heartbreaking not to be able to care for him in the way 3 year olds need to be cared for. When he screamed, I would try to pick him up, just like I had done with every 3 year old in my care- relatives and students alike. He could not allow himself to be comforted. It was terrible for me to have to see a child upset, and not be able to comfort him. I think that was one of the hardest things for me to have to cope with. Helplessness would become a very common feeling for me, but it was unbearable to have my attempts to soothe cause further discontent.

Best Interest?

I agreed to meet the former grandmother with the boys in a public setting, and the first time she backed out. I wish I had never set it up in the first place. It was just 3 days after the guardianship began. She said she was sick. Then she sent me a text that week about a T-Ball ceremony that I had only just found out about from the former grandfather. I had an appointment, and I told her that he wouldn't be going. I didn't have any time to give notice to cancel my appointment, and honestly- meeting up with her, her husband and the boys didn't sound like a great plan. She had not attended any T-Ball games that season, and James couldn't name a single kid on the team. James didn't want to go, and it would have been hard to arrange it since I had an appointment. We opted out. This upset her immensely, but she backed off for about a week. For some reason, she sent me some provocative photos (posted online somewhere) of the Superman lady that her husband was friends with, and then requested to have the boys overnight. I said "no", because I was bringing the boys to see their birthmother (a mistake, I realized later, but at the time I thought was a good idea). We were also going school shopping, as the new school year was set to begin in about a week. She was irate at the thought of her daughter getting to see them. I wish she wasn't right about the visit being a bad idea, but her reasons were way off anyway. Regardless, she wanted them Sunday- both of them- which was not a typical request during the time when they lived with their former grandfather. I had seen an advertisement for a special back-to-school event at the zoo, and told her we had plans to go, but extended an invitation for her to attend with us. I expected her to back out, but as my luck would have it, she didn't.

We had found out by this time that the former grandfather had indeed filed for guardianship. Our knowledge of the laws regarding this type of child custody/guardianship was extremely limited. I was worried that he could show up with some kind of papers and take the boys. I was terrified, and tried to let the boys know that if anything happened and they had to go back, I was going to get the "grown-up papers" to fix it as soon as I could. We started talking about "grown-up papers" a lot. That was how I referred to anything that came from the court that made things safe. There were a lot of "What if?" questions, but none too realistic. I remember being so scared that someone would come with legal papers and take the boys, but I never made any mention of that to them, other than reassuring them that I would do whatever I needed to in order to be the one to take care of them. I actually think they worried about that more than they let on, even without a big discussion of the matter.

There was supposed to be a person- a guardian ad litem- to make sure that the guardianship was in the boys' best interest. I thought that someone would check things out. I worked really hard to get a decent bedroom set up for the boys. I bought a new bunk bed, new mattresses, new bed sets, and even some border for the wall to help make them feel good about their new home, and have some sense of belonging. I made sure to get their input for some wall stickers (dinosaurs for James, trucks for Jackson). While I was building their bed, I had them set up to watch TV. That was about the only activity they typically did without

24

difficulty. I checked on them frequently, and my parents were in the home, too. I thought things were fine. I only left them out of sight (not earshot) for about 10 minutes at a time. I was running myself ragged going back and forth. I thought I was being overly paranoid, but when I discovered their actions on one of my "checks"- I was appalled. They had built a long stick out of this wooden construction set that was at my parents' house. They were using it to poke at and torment my pet rabbit that was in his hutch. I realize that any children might have done that, but there was something different about the look that James had on his face. There was no remorse, no embarrassment, no understanding of why it was a problem, or why I would be upset. Jackson, on the other hand, seemed to immediately feel sorry for what he had done. He was startled when I found them, but when I said "You may *not* hurt animals", it seemed to sink in that what he was doing was hurtful. I could be giving him too much credit, but he seemed to be upset with himself, not upset because he had gotten in trouble. James didn't really have any reaction. He immediately said that he didn't do it, even though I saw him. He didn't seem to care at all. I don't even think he was upset that I got after them. I was scared to leave them even semi-unattended after that. I got an internet camera so I could monitor them better in the future when I needed to be in a different room. It was definitely a worthwhile expense, and I still need it to this day. As for the guardian ad litem, she never came. I needed to get a bedroom in order for the boys anyway, but the urgency to get things completely set wouldn't have been hanging over my head. She was supposed to come twice and cancelled. I never even saw the woman until the second hearing, where she would state that the former grandfather was perfectly capable, and that the boys should be able to visit him unsupervised. She came to this conclusion from a telephone conversation with him!!

The Zoo

When it came time to go to the zoo with the former grandmother, I was getting extremely suspicious of her intentions. I had begun to believe that her reason for being with the boys was simply to flaunt her control to her husband. She wanted to drive together, which I wasn't very comfortable with. I did have her meet me at our child care center rather than her home so I wouldn't have my car parked there for her husband to see. It was a very uncomfortable experience from start to finish. On the drive in, when I told the boys we were meeting "Nana", Jackson went into a complete fit. He screamed and slipped out of his car seat. I had waited to tell them because she had already stood us up once, and at that point, I didn't realize the total fear of her that they had. I actually didn't want them to think poorly of her if she did stand them up again. The reality of the relationship was completely different than what I assumed it was. Even though Jackson screamed when going near her house, I thought that it was just because he didn't want to stay with her- not because he was terrified of her. My rose-colored glasses let me see that he wanted to be with me, rather than her. I still wasn't understanding that the boys had been harmed so severely. I tried to explain that we were all going together, she was just coming, but he was not easily consoled. When we arrived, he turned it off and copied James as he gave "Nana" a hug. And so we began the adventure of a lifetime. The zoo was nearly an hour away. When we got there, she put on her big white sunhat, dug out 3 brand-new pairs of sunglasses from her console, and asked me which I thought were best for each boy. I gave her my suggestions, not disclosing my opinion of the very feminine frog ones with the pink bows. I simply stated that I thought they'd like the other ones. She opened the back of her vehicle (we took hers because she had a brand-new wagon she thought we needed to use). There, with the plastic still on the canopy, was a wagon. It took her 15 minutes to figure out how to get the canopy on. I finally assisted somewhat, and it took everything I had to avoid laughing out loud at the sight.

Here we were, at the zoo at the end of summer. Her skin hadn't seen the sun at all. It was just as white as her enormous sunhat. The boys, ages 6 and 3 were both crammed into this wagon that would have been tight for children 2 years younger. I told myself that I was NOT going to pull that silly wagon with those kids in it. She buckled them in (well, attempted to- if I recall correctly, the little seat belt wouldn't fit around James), and began to pull. I watched, wondering how long it would last. I assumed she would kick the kids out and make them walk like the other children their ages at the zoo. I bring a group of preschoolers to that very zoo every year, and even the young ones walk it. It's a nice zoo, and has a fair amount of walking, but the layout makes it pretty easy. Regardless, we were off, wagon in tow. She took pictures at every exhibit. I took a few, too. Jackson looks miserable in every one, and James had on his goofy grin that I now know is only shown when he has anxiety. That crazy woman made it pulling that wagon for about 20 minutes. She was groaning and moaning. I felt a bit guilty about not offering to help, but I was sticking with it. I was NOT going to pull that wagon. I should have relented. I shouldn't have been so mean. I don't think it would have prevented what happened next, but who knows? She finally broke down and asked me to pull the wagon. She told me she just couldn't do it anymore. I said I would, of course, but in my head I was wishing I had the courage to tell her that I thought the kids could probably walk. Even though I had intended to never pull that stupid thing, I couldn't say "no" when asked directly to help.

At that very moment, she brought out her drinks she had smuggled into the zoo for the kids. I was grateful when I saw that they weren't juice boxes with straws, because I knew that the zoo banned them due to an animal injury. I almost wish they had been, though, because the alternative was worse. She had apple juice. Not little child-size drinks- it was apple juice in large bottles. She offered them the juice, and of course the boys were more than happy for a drink. I was going to offer water, but didn't think that the apple juice was a problem anyway. The first bottle probably wasn't. I didn't really think they needed another one, but I didn't know what to say. "Nana" would have had a fit if I didn't permit the boys the drinks she brought. The boys wouldn't have been happy, either. I let it go, but was thinking that 2 large bottles of straight apple juice might be excessive. When the 3rd bottle was offered and accepted, I was worried. She gave me an odd look while giving them the last bottle, but I thought that maybe it was in response to my expression, which was likely odd, too, as I witnessed the 3rd bottles of apple juice for each child being opened (and spilled on the floor, for we were in an indoor exhibit). I was arguing with myself, thinking maybe I was just wrong in assuming that too much juice would cause some problems. I had, after all, never been a mother. I wasn't a mother yet, and she was. I began to resign myself to the fact that I didn't know everything and that it was fine. Surely she knew them well enough to know that they could drink lots of apple juice and be fine.

She had fresh grapes in her cooler for a snack on the way home. So, after eating breakfast, my boys had 3 bottles of apple juice and grapes until just after noon. Jackson started saying he had to go to the bathroom about halfway home. "Nana" hit me with her demands at about that same time. Jackson was crying because he needed to go to the bathroom, James was making weird noises and laughing at Jackson because he was screaming about the bathroom, and "Nana" was asking me why I wouldn't let her have them for the weekends. It was quite overwhelming. I thought that we would never get back. She thought that this zoo trip made everything cool. We were buddies, apparently, and I'd just let the kids go with her. I reminded her that we had plans for the weekend, and that it had only been 3 weeks. She had declined to meet the first weekend, didn't ask for the second, and here we were for the 3rd. It wasn't as if I had been completely avoiding her, although I would have liked to. She was pretty put out with me, and put on a fake loving departure ceremony as she left. The boys weren't even looking at her, so she took their faces and kissed them.

By this time, Jackson was really screaming about needing a bathroom. I had to go to my sister's house anyway to take care of her pets because she was out of town, so we went there and Jackson made it to the bathroom. James never said a word, and didn't try to use the bathroom as I had suggested. Before the day was out, however, he had soiled several pairs of pants. I didn't know it at the time, but James had issues with bowel control- or rather, his desire to maintain control, no matter what his body needed to do. The apple juice episode allowed him to conceal this problem from me for another couple of weeks, as his bowel was empty. He could then maintain his control for another long stretch of time. I asked the boys if "Nana" usually gave them apple juice, and I never got an answer I could believe completely, so I don't really know if she did or not. I explained that a little bit of juice is fine, but drinking 3 bottles of apple juice would give anyone tummy trouble. It was a really long time before they would drink apple juice again. When I would give them juice, they were scared and asked "Is that apple juice?" It took about a year before they wouldn't question juice. They still talk about it. It was definitely a memorable event. I didn't know it then, but apple juice was only mildly harmful compared to the lasting effects of the trip to the zoo that day.

Expectations

At this point, the former grandmother was acting crazy, but not to the extent that her actions took over my life completely. She sent me texts frequently, making the same requests again and again.   Then came orientation at school for James. She had criticized my decision to give James a fresh start at a new school, but wanted to go to the orientation. I avoided her question about the time of the event for a while, a cowardly attempt to avoid confrontation. When she badgered me enough about it, I finally said that it really wasn't a thing for grandparents. When she became very upset at that statement, I reminded her that she didn't have anything to do with his last school experience (with a little nudge from my sister to "say it like it is"). That sent her into a complete tailspin. She texted, she emailed, she called. It was scary, actually. Her lengthy email very clearly stated what I was going to do: let her have the kids every weekend from a certain time on Saturday and pick them up at a certain time on Sunday. I was not going to take them to do anything with my family: the boys already had a family. It gave a deadline for my response "or else"- meaning she wouldn't "support me at the hearing". It was quite a message. Statements like "this is non-negotiable" and "I'm not accepting this answer again" were scattered throughout her email. She said she was going to attend the orientation anyway and "shame on" me if I didn't go just to avoid her. Her deadline for my response was 5:30. At about 4:40, I got a phone call. The caller ID displayed phone numbers that were similar to our 2nd line from our child care center, so I unknowingly answered the call from her, thinking it was a call from our work phone. My mouth went dry when I heard the familiar voice. It was a sappy sweet tone. "Did you get my email?" the voice said. Really? She had written all that negative stuff, sent it with a 'read receipt' to be certain it was delivered, and then called me to sweetly ask if I got it. I said I had, and that the orientation was really just for those responsible for the day-to-day things, like picking up, dropping off, homework, bringing classroom supplies, and making sure that we knew the class expectations. It wasn't like a program or performance intended for extended family. She said "I see how this is going to be, I'm going to take care of this right now", and hung up.

I was terrified going to the school that evening. She didn't show, but I was worried she would. Here I was, being a first-time "parent", enrolling my kid in school, having to explain our odd situation, and having to be on the lookout for a crazy woman. I was so nervous I was sweating through my clothes. I remember hoping that nobody could tell how distraught I was. I saw many parents of my students there, people I worked with in the past, and former students of all ages. I still don't know if I looked as upset as I was.

Even though the crazy woman didn't show, she wasted no time in requesting the boys again. I was actually still at the orientation when the texts began. She told me what time to bring the boys by that Saturday. Once I got home, I responded to her multiple texts by offering her a time to meet up at a park again, and asked her to stop harassing me. That's when I was told "Don't start any of this drama with me, young lady," and "I'm not harassing you, and you know it!" It was already nearly 9:00 at night, and I had been dealing with calls, texts, and emails all day long. I stopped responding, and she finally let up for a day or two.

I was avoiding her calls, but she started calling my sister's number, and my parents' house, too. She again requested the boys for the weekend I had already declined. We had plans to be out of town. She sent texts all weekend long, and tried calling my number, my sister's number- everything. She was really going nuts. She sent the same text 3 times within 90 minutes while I was driving back from our weekend trip. When I got home and received yet another text as I walked in the door- saying the same thing- "Are the boys ok? Did my daughter say she'd call me?"- I was done. Enough was enough! I asked her again to leave me alone, which only caused another flood of texts. She finally requested to meet up as I had suggested countless times. She did not attend the hearing that she implied she would come to with the intent to share with the judge how awful I was. We met at the park, with my brother-in-law parked nearby.

My whole family had become concerned with her unpredictable behavior and threatening attitude. I was grateful that someone I could trust was nearby, just in case. She brought 4 treat bags (all the same, two for each child) from James's birthday party several months before- ones that she had not actually remembered to bring to the party. I had to console Jackson prior to the meeting, only to have signs of visible distress disappear as soon she came into sight. James was just going along with whatever.

This is where many of my mistakes with the kids began. I kept asking them whether they liked going with "Nana" and "Papa", and whether they wanted to visit. I shouldn't have done that. The answers I got, for the most part, were that they *didn't* want to see them. That was mostly from James. Jackson would just scream and not talk about it. Then, at the park, James also had to deal with "Nana" badgering him about wanting to go to her house to visit. He looked very uncomfortable, shrugged, and really didn't even speak an answer, but she acted as if he had said that he *did* want to visit her. She left the park with a smug grin on her face. When we got to the car, I asked him about what he really wanted, and he couldn't give a straight answer. He said he didn't really want to go, but then went back and forth. That's when I said that I was just going to make the decision anyway, which is what I should have done in the first place. He was a confused 6 year old going through a big life change, and didn't need to have to make those decisions. I really wish I had been smart enough to figure that out *before* I asked him the same questions so many times. I was trying so hard to make the right choices, and I felt like the kids should have some say in the matter. They didn't need that- they had no idea what they wanted or needed. What they needed was an adult to take care of them. If I had it to do over, I would have never even asked their input about who to see, or how they felt about visiting with family.

The former grandmother didn't wait an hour before she sent me a text that evening, complete with details about the times I was to drop off and pick up the boys that weekend. I said "no", but offered to meet up again. She was livid. Her onslaught of texts was enough to drive anyone mad. I didn't respond to all of them, but made clear from time to time that I would be happy to arrange a time to meet up for a visit. She kept it up- all through the night and early in the morning. No response from me simply evoked multiple texts stating "I expect answers to my questions".

I was getting pretty frustrated with all of this, especially with the lies she started telling. She even made up things that could not possibly have been true- such as communication with her daughter, visitation demands through the court (at least at that time, she hadn't gone that far yet), and other off-the-wall tales that I assume intended to scare me into providing her access to the kids. There were also attempts to gain sympathy for her divorce situation. She would go on about how terrible her husband was, and how she was going to have to get her own cell phone plan. She was upset because the judge didn't consider internet and cable a necessity that the husband would need to continue to pay.

I'm not sure why she thought I could relate to all of that mess. I thought she was getting a pretty good deal, if all she was having to pay for was internet, cable, and a cell phone plan, while her husband had to pay all of the other bills- the house, utilities, and the payments for both vehicles she drove. Between the two former grandparents, there were 4 vehicles. The boys' birthmother told me that they each had a vehicle for winter, and a vehicle for summer. I had a hard time feeling pity for her financial state when she had a large house to herself, paid for by her husband, and two vehicles to drive. I found her whining humorous and disgusting at the same time. Although I was glad when the pleas for pity would cease, it was really the lesser of two evils. The pity party was replaced by demands- complete with instructions for when and where I was to drop the boys off and pick them up.

Everything Starts Out Little

I had to keep reminding myself that I had hardly had the boys a month. It wasn't as if I were hiding, or like they were used to seeing the former grandmother frequently. The weekend trip I had taken that she was so upset about was to my brother's house. His wife had planned a fundraiser party for my niece for a band trip. It was the first time the boys had ever stayed in a hotel, so it was definitely an experience. I was certainly not creating distance to insult her, and honestly their behavior didn't exactly make the trip all that fun, anyway. It was memorable, without question, but fun... that's not a word I would use to describe that first out of town overnight trip. I would discover later that anything new and different would cause embarrassing behavior without fail. We survived, however.

I'm not sure if all of the creatures residing at my brother's house did, though. I guess James decided that it would be cool to try and drown all of the little toads hopping around the yard by putting them in the backyard pool. My brother yelled at first, but later, he calmly tried to explain why they couldn't do that. It was a significant event to the boys, and even though my brother isn't a scary guy, that one incident sticks in their minds because he yelled. They *did* need to stop. Harming animals is never acceptable, and James gave the appearance of being giddy putting those things in the water. I didn't know that yelling was one of those things that they couldn't handle, and I didn't view my brother's actions as too extreme. It was brief, mostly just saying "stop!", and "don't ever do that again". If my brother had known that yelling was something that upset them more than just about anything, I don't think he'd have done it. He didn't threaten them, hit them, or even touch them at all, but they are still working to be able to be near him without displaying behaviors that I now realize are related to anxiety.

My brother might have inadvertently frightened the boys once, but I was adding to my list of damaging mistakes, probably on a daily- if not hourly- basis. There are countless things I did or allowed to happen that made things worse. I was unknowingly contributing to further trauma, while attempting to control the behaviors that the boys were using to communicate their needs. I expected them to use their large vocabulary and speak to me about their problems. I didn't realize that they were using a different language- their actions. I was not understanding what they so blatantly told me through their behaviors. I thought that the boys *needed* to see their birthmother. I thought that a good relationship had been established, and expected to maintain a relationship after her release. I knew it would be different, but I thought that being able to spend time together would be fine. The boys' behavior was erratic at any given time, but the visits to the birthmother were unbearable. They would go completely crazy! This was after the hour long drive to get there that would take us 2 hours sometimes.

Jackson was typically distraught in the car, but those trips were the worst. He did have trouble in the car for every trip- short, long, on the way to somewhere, on the way home- it didn't matter. I didn't think that the purpose for the trip made much difference at the time, and I guess I'll never really know. The length of the trip contributed to the difficulty, for sure.

Shamefully, I tried everything I could think of to get Jackson's screaming under control. We stopped at nearly every exit. I tried bribing with candy and ice cream, threatening with loss of toys (which was a joke- they hardly had any, and didn't know how to play), begging, pleading, yelling, even spanking. I tried waiting him out. James and I once stood on the side of the road at an exit on the interstate for 20 minutes, just waiting for Jackson to stop screaming. He had a high-pitched, blood curdling scream that somehow, without any loss of volume or shrillness, could go on for hours. He could scream for nearly a minute without even taking a breath. We did the waiting game for a while, until Jackson got the better of me. He would stop screaming. I would open the door. He would begin again. It didn't take me long to figure out that this 3 year old had outwitted me. He had won. I don't know how we survived those trips.

While visiting, I didn't think that they gave the appearance of being sad or scared, but they were all over the place. They were more hyper than any kids I had ever seen. James would climb on things, jump, do odd things that were aggravating like throwing food, trying to jump on his birthmother, and just be loud and obnoxious. Jackson would follow suit. It was exhausting for me, but what was worse was the fact that I was re-traumatizing them every time we went to visit. I had no idea.

We also had to take the hour long drive to get to the first therapist we went to. My sister went with us for the first appointment. The boys went wild. I was in such a state of disbelief at their behavior that I didn't even know what to say. The therapist asked all sorts of questions about their background and what we knew about them. I was ashamed that I wasn't very confident in my responses about the boys' behavior, even to fill out the paperwork. I knew them before the guardianship, yes, but I had only been taking care of them for a few weeks. I didn't know nearly enough about them to provide information about patterns of behavior.

While in the therapist's room, they were having to hear a lot of stuff that I'm sure was uncomfortable for them to listen to. They cleared out the toy shelves, wrestled on the floor, took stuff off the therapist's desk, threw things around the room, went under the furniture, and were extremely disruptive, to say the least. James was completely out of control. He was standing right in front of my face as I began to speak, blocking my view of the therapist. I had been gently telling the boys to quit doing things, giving suggestions for different activities, but nothing worked. Just when I thought that they could not possibly be any more disruptive- it got worse. James chewed on a very large stuffed snake, which I thought was really disgusting. Then he smacked me in the face with that slobbery, wet snake.

Finally, the therapist asked what I would typically do if the boys were acting like they were. I said that they usually didn't, but if we were in a setting that I felt in control of, that all of the toys would have been taken away from them. She asked why I hadn't done that, and after an initial (embarrassing) reply of "I don't know, exactly", I said that I didn't know how to react in that situation, and there had been little guidance for the boys about which toys were available to play with. Although I didn't tell her, it had seemed to me until then, that she thought that it was fine for them to trash the room. Then I felt like I was the idiot for not stopping them. I don't know how I could have, though. I did not have the right words to say to help them make good choices. They were truly out of control. The whole experience was miserable.

We went back to therapy the following week without my sister, but it wasn't any better. I remember the therapist asking "So what exactly are you wanting me to do?" I tried to explain that these children had switched homes abruptly, and their whole lives had been changed. They were likely abused, and certainly neglected. She told me that they needed time to adjust. She implied that some of the behaviors were related more to the change in lifestyle, rather than due to certain neglect or abuse. The toileting issues, for example- might have been related to the fact that they had lived in a camper, and using the bathroom might have been discouraged. She had little concern with the fact that the children didn't bathe regularly in the past. She related that, too, to the type of home they had been living in. After asking what I was trying to do as far as improve their behavior, she commended my methods. She thought it was especially great that I had purchased scooters for them, and Jackson's was in the trunk of the car until we could take a few car trips without screaming. She may have thought that it was a great idea, but I, after driving an hour listening to that child's shrill scream, would have liked something that was going to work. I hadn't had any success yet. I think we went back there once more, but without a treatment plan, there wasn't much point.

Their behavior was certainly worse during any kind of appointment. I brought them for a physical, and they acted so nutty that the doctor returned to the room with a list of psychologists that worked with children. I did call many of them, but none were willing to see Jackson, since he was only 3, and were not very open to seeing James, either. I didn't have a lot to say about the trouble we were having, as it was all new. I just had a feeling that they needed professional support to help them adapt to their new lives.

When I called, the medical professionals I spoke with seemed to imply that the behaviors I described were normal. Not one suggested that the life experiences I described warranted therapy. I still felt that we needed support, and over the next several months, would try different places, and be given the same response. I couldn't pinpoint any specific problems to inform them of. There were weird issues, but nothing that appeared serious on the surface. Little incidents bothered me, like the reaction to the shirt James had worn the day I got him. Other things, too, like the fact that Jackson wouldn't get out of bed without James being awake, were troublesome to me. He would wake up, and I'd quietly try to get him to come out and let James sleep. He would not come. They were too easy to put to bed. I didn't have *any* trouble with putting them to bed. This, while somewhat concerning, was a blessing. I don't know how I would have made it if we struggled with bedtime all of the time. Jackson went through phases where he would stall or be demanding, but overall, they went to bed, and continued to do so without a lot of trouble. The other thing that struck me as odd was their lack of whining over needing food. What kind of kid *never* says that they are hungry? The only time I ever heard "I'm hungry" was right after I fed them, which seemed odd. Later I would discover that the "I'm hungry" comments were only right after I'd fed them, *and* when other people could hear them. It was not a true expression of a need, after all. They never expressed hunger, and even when I asked, or said it was time to eat, they would seem upset and not want to eat. I still haven't quite come to a complete understanding about that, but I believe that it has something to do with their lack of ability to regulate their own bodies. They just can't feel the same way most people do. When I thought of what to say when calling these therapists, the idea of saying "My kids go to bed too easily, and never say they're hungry," seemed laughable. Who *wouldn't* want their kids to do those things? Although I saw each of these things as concerns, they weren't really problems that seemed to justify the need for professional intervention.

The Craziness Saga

The issues with the former grandmother did not let up. She was relentless. I didn't know what to do. She was incredibly annoying, and it wasn't like I didn't have enough to deal with. The boys were adjusting, but their behavior could be difficult and unpredictable. They actually were very pleasant much of the time originally, but as time went on, challenging behaviors began to surface. Jackson was more of a problem, at first. The screaming in the car was terrible, and he would have fits frequently. I worked really hard with Jackson to get him to let me be near him. I used some things I'd learned from early childhood conferences like little games that encouraged touch. I read books to gain insight. When I started the activities, he would only let me play the little games with his sock monkey. It took days before he'd let me start the little rhyme with him without touch, and it was another 2 weeks before he let me do the whole thing with him. It wasn't anything big, just moving our hands around together, and singing a little rhyme. That really was the breakthrough event for him, though. Once he let me do that, I could pick him up or sit with him to read, even though it didn't really feel natural. I was still unsuccessful in comforting him, but progress was beginning. He transformed from an untouchable child into an incredibly demanding one. He was capable of dressing himself, but insisted on having me dress him. I went back and forth on my feelings about that issue. At first, I was just thrilled that he wanted me to do anything. Then, in the evenings, I wanted him to do it himself so I could finish getting stuff ready for bed- put toothpaste on toothbrushes, pick a book, and get clothes ready for the morning. In the morning, it was faster to dress the half-asleep child, so I didn't mind that routine. I don't actually remember when he started dressing himself again completely, but it was well into our second year together. It was not the most pressing concern in our lives. During all of this adjustment and relationship development, I was dealing with serious craziness and multiple court hearings.

The second guardianship hearing was, by far, the craziest experience ever. It was a circus, even without the former grandmother there. The former grandfather was there, and was actually sort of approachable. I still think he had abused the boys, and at the very least neglected them and caused trauma due to the events that the boys witnessed while in his care. He, however, seemed to agree that the boys needed a better place to be. He didn't think that the camper was a good enough home, and he wasn't really the best person to be a primary caregiver. I still feel bad for him the way it happened, but I don't have any guilt about doing what had to be done to get the boys taken care of. At the hearing, there were several witnesses on his behalf, and the Superman lady that our attorney had subpoenaed was present. She was the one responsible for the middle of the night joyride that started the whole thing. The campground owner testified that the former grandfather was a wonderful caregiver, and that was about it. The Superman lady was a sight. Even the former grandfather held his face in his hands as she went on the stand. She carried one of her high heels rather than wearing it, had grown-out dreadlocks in her long blonde hair, and wore an orange hunting cap with "LOIS LANE" written on it in permanent marker. Really- you can't make stuff like that up! She had come to talk to my sister and me before the hearing and had told us how the former grandfather owed her money, and how she worked for the CIA, and that the bank was in on some conspiracy thing, and that her sound system was keeping her informed about the events to come. It was hard to listen to without laughing or running away. It was really scary. I had never met anyone so crazy in all my life, and I don't think I ever will.

When she was called up to the stand, she gave the information requested- spelled her name, and gave her address, while adding a lot of irrelevant information. Our attorney asked about the incidents we knew about that had involved her. Jackson had knocked a truck out of gear at a park while they were under her supervision which resulted in damage of a park bench and trash can, as well as a police report. It's unclear whether the former grandfather was present during the time of the wreck. There was also that infamous middle-of-the-night joyride.

How the topic shifted, I cannot remember. I recall her being asked about her whereabouts during another incident, and she said that she was not available during that time. Upon further questioning, she responded with the fact that she was committed during that time because she is a lunatic. She didn't just say "lunatic", she spelled it- "L-U-N-A-T-I-C". It was about this time that her speech about some government involvement began, and a monologue covering her perception of the former grandfather (negative, at this point), and about some financial problems he had supposedly caused for her. The judge was actually using the gavel by this time, demanding order in the court, and she was asked to step down. She was assisted to a seat in the courtroom by the court officers.

The former grandfather went to speak next, but I can't remember much of what he said, as the Superman lady was mumbling things behind me, and I was a nervous wreck. When I came up to the stand, the Superman lady caused such a scene that the judge had her removed from the courtroom. I had been asked about my reasons for concern about the boys being in the former grandfather's care, and I stated that the company he kept was worrisome to me. She knew I was talking about her, and she stood up and started shouting things- nothing that made much sense. I was such a wreck at that point that I probably couldn't have made sense of much of anything, but she seemed irrational anyway. The court officers returned a few minutes later to retrieve the Hello Kitty purse she'd left on the bench. I don't recall much of what I said during that time, but my time on the stand was interrupted yet again. About 5 minutes after the purse had been returned to her, the Superman lady barged through the door of the courtroom claiming to be the attorney for the boys' birthmother. It was quite a scene. I would not have believed it if I hadn't seen it myself.

The rest of the time I spent on the stand was slightly less dramatic. I testified to the screams of my boys upon going down the street towards the camper, of the clothing that they wore that was 3 sizes too small, the shoes 2 sizes too small, and of the suspected abuse. I had to back off of the abuse because although our center (and the public school) had made several reports of neglect and physical abuse, I had no evidence of the sexual abuse- just a suspicion. My claim that sexual abuse was a possibility, even though I was clear that there was not much to go on, gave me an uneasy feeling. I am a mandated reporter, and even though we'd made reports, the sexual abuse was not specifically mentioned when we had provided the information. My knowledge of accusations by his stepdaughter 20 years prior had little to do with accusing him of such acts with the boys now. The accusations by his stepdaughter were never substantiated, although I believe them to be true. The only thing I had to base my suspicion on was the fact that Jackson refused to be nude in front of anyone. He had to change alone when they got into swimming suits at our child care center. Typically, 3 year old boys really don't care if someone comes into the room while they change. This was not enough to substantiate any abuse claim, even though reports had been made for other abuse and neglect incidents. The state had investigated the family several times, but no evidence of abuse was ever determined to be found. Red marks were gone by the time the abuse allegations were investigated, and the "standard of living" was acceptable, according to those responsible for investigating.

The outcome of the hearing, even with the Superman lady being presented as the former grandfather's choice of company, was not as positive as we had hoped. We were to maintain guardianship, but visitation was granted to the former grandfather. Although he had the right to demand to have them every other Saturday, he never requested to have them alone. During the times we did meet, he wasn't nearly as difficult to be around as the former grandmother.

Every time I thought we were comfortable for a day or so, the former grandmother would start up again. What really set her into crazy mode was after the hearing that granted the former grandfather visitation. He never actually acted on it, but met once at a park and attended a couple of flag football games. She thought that he was having visitation and she wasn't, so her jealousy made her become obsessed with getting the boys alone and overnight. I still declined, and she finally settled for meeting me at a park. She was pretty displeased about it, as was I. I don't know if I really should have done what I did that day, but it started a whole mess of problems. Even though it seemed like this had been going on for a long time, the boys had only been with me for about 6 weeks. I'd arranged for her to meet us a couple of times, and we'd done the horrible zoo trip. She hadn't seen Jackson in months before the Superman joyride, and James had only been there that one time in the past 4 months. The sudden desire to have this imagined relationship was getting to be really difficult to keep up with.

The day we were to meet with the former grandmother, I was exhausted. It is always a hard week- we start our preschool year the day after Labor Day. We spend the week prior getting things switched from school-age materials and equipment back to preschool, planning for the year, and getting paperwork in order. I had really been getting frustrated with her relentless texting and negative remarks. I don't know what gave me the inspiration to back out, but I did it. I told her I was tired, and just didn't want to deal with the negativity that day. The kids and I didn't need that. I did offer to meet another day that week, I just really didn't want to do it that day.

I had apologized for canceling, but she was not taking it well. It really sparked her ire, and the flood of texts came in. She accused me of needing anger management, and hiding things. It bothered me some, and I was becoming really frustrated with her annoying texts, but I could still handle it. What came next went too far. The next day she barged right on into our early childhood center, and demanded to see Jackson. He was visible in a classroom, and she approached him and brought him upstairs. Thankfully, my mother and sister protected him and were able to keep him there. My classroom is in another building, so I was unaware of any problem until after it had happened. I am told that Jackson was clawing to get away from her, but she carried him to the front door. At this time, he was not comfortable with touch from much of anyone, and would only allow *me* to hold him sometimes. The people who witnessed the incident have said that as soon as she put him down when she got upstairs, he ran to my nephew, who was 15 at the time. He sought comfort in my nephew, which is especially profound, since Jackson would not seek out physical closeness with my nephew or anyone else but me, even two years later.

That crazy woman had car seats in her car, and was waiting for James to return from school. My mom and sister made sure that James was kept safe during the after school transition, and brought him to me. The former grandmother lied about the events that day- even under oath! She stated that Jackson wanted to go with her, and that everyone was really happy that she was there. My mother, a very quiet and non-confrontational person, made it clear to her that she had already had her chance. She asked "Where were you for the last 10 months when they were living in the camper?" I am so grateful for her support, and I am quite sure that it shocked the former grandmother, as she could not come up with a response. I just couldn't believe that the former grandmother could be so brazen. How could she feel confident enough to walk into our center and approach my little boy? I know it wasn't kind of me to cancel our arranged meeting time the day before, but she had seen my boys more in the last 3 weeks than she had in the past year. The desire to create a relationship with the boys didn't take place until they finally had a safe place to be. It may sound like I was excessively harsh, but I didn't trust her then, and I don't trust her today. I filed an order for protection the following day.

That night, Jackson was a mess. When I came to pick him up, he actually clutched me. He grabbed on and didn't let go. The same child that avoided my physical touch was now clinging to me with all the strength he had. I had to pry him off of me to get him in the car. He said nothing. At supper, he went by the sliding glass door in the room where we were eating, and curled up in a ball, still silent. He wouldn't come to supper. He wouldn't speak. My dad even asked what was wrong with him. When he was told, away from the boys, my dad's face showed sadness rather than the anger I had expected. He saw the hurt in my little boy, and that overpowered the feeling of anger towards that woman.

Jackson's rash began the next day. He started licking his lips and wiping his face above his lip constantly. I took a video of the boys for their birthmother (I thought I could send one, but it wasn't permitted). He wiped his face in that 30 second video nonstop. I couldn't even count the number of times. It was terrible. His little red mustache became so raw that he couldn't even eat. He would start screaming as the food touched his lips. I read up and found that nipple cream for nursing mothers might work. I had to put it on him after he was asleep. He would be raw by the afternoon again. I started doing it once he went to sleep, and again before he woke up. He wouldn't let me do it while he was awake. The rash became less obvious, but he had it for 3 months straight. When I thought it was gone, she of course did something else to help it return. It was 6 months before it was gone for good.

Rubbing tags was his other attempt at soothing himself. He would rub the tag in the back of his pajama pants, until I finally started putting them on backwards so he didn't have to contort himself to reach. He still puts them on backwards sometimes.

The Next Step

There was an added complication that arose during our first months together, as well. The half-sister of the boys' birthmother was in contact with her stepfather (the boys' former grandfather), the same stepfather she had accused of sexually abusing her years before. The same stepfather that, along with her mother, had relinquished parental rights by choice when she was 12 years old. She came to one of the flag football games. It was awkward. The boys didn't seem to know her, but she acted like she knew them. She didn't even know their ages, and appeared shocked when Jackson spoke. She said that she didn't know he could talk. I would not have recognized her if she hadn't introduced herself. Even knowing who she was, I had to look really hard to find any resemblance to the young girl I once knew. The only word that begins to describe her is "rough". Her teeth were damaged and some were missing. Her skin looked unnatural. It was blotchy, and paired with her expressionless face, it looked as if she had a rubber mask on. She was polite, especially at first. I couldn't figure out what to say to her. I knew she'd given birth to some children, but she had given them up. I knew that while working for a carnival, she had married and divorced. I'd heard that she had gotten into drugs, which her appearance confirmed. Our lives couldn't have gone in more opposite directions from the time

I had known her as a child. I felt sorry for her, but was not feeling that becoming friends with her would be an option. She was upset that her half-sister had chosen me to take care of her kids. She admitted that she had no contact with her, and no means to take care of children, and no job, and no real home (she was living with a boyfriend- also unemployed, unless you count illegal activity as a job). She told me that she wanted to start a relationship with the boys.

I admired her honesty, especially in comparison to the interactions I'd had with the former grandmother. At least she admitted that the relationship would be beginning rather than pretending that a close one had been established. I gave her an honest, yet deceptively optimistic response- I said that we were really busy, but maybe we could work something out later. She called a few times, but I think she became really irritated that I didn't make more of an effort to meet. I truly was busy, and although I should have been a bit more straightforward with her, I didn't want to make it a priority. We had enough complications without adding anyone else to the mix. I was trying to put it off to see if things would work out, but I think I knew that it never would. I regret not being direct and saying "no" from the start.

At this point, we were still thinking that guardianship was the final route. A petition for grandparent visitation from the former grandmother came into play, as well as continued harassment and court hearings regarding the protection order. After a short discussion, we decided that adoption would be the solution to the problem, as it severed all rights of grandparents. The arrangements for the permanent care of the boys had already been established, so the adoption was just a formality. The birthmother was actually really pleased with this idea; we had agreed upon the long-term care for the boys from the beginning. She said that she had wanted it that way from the start. I really wish we'd done it that way, too. By this time, the estimate of $1,500-$2,500 had been met and exceeded by about 5 times that amount. At the end of this whole ordeal, the costs exceeded 10 times the highest estimate during our attorney consultation. I had borrowed from my mom, gotten a loan co-signed by my dad, and had blown through every bit of money I had. I am still struggling, as the costs were astronomical.

We were still going for visits to the birthmother pretty much every Saturday. It was an extremely unpleasant adventure every time. I had to start using a 5-point harness car seat with Jackson, because even though he met the weight requirement for the booster I had bought, he would slide out every time he got mad. I had to use the child lock on the door, and the window lock, too. Just thinking about those car trips makes me feel sick. James didn't say anything about not wanting to go, but he occasionally became carsick, or so I thought. A few of our trips we had to turn around because he got sick on the way. I now realize that he has no problems with motion sickness. He only gets sick when he is upset over something. While supporting the relationship between the boys and their birthmother seemed like a good idea, it was likely one of the more damaging mistakes that I made. My intentions were good, but hindsight allows me to see the reality of the situation. Good intentions cannot negate the consequences of the decisions I made, but denial can't either. I can only continue on with good intentions, recognize my past mistakes, and strive to do the best that I can with the knowledge I have.

The first trip to visit after their birthmother had consented to the adoption was the worst. Jackson screamed the entire way-even with many stops to try and get him to quiet down. James was in a bad mood. Who wouldn't be after listening to screaming for over an hour? They behaved in their typical horrid fashion while I tried to get signed in. They would run around, touch the metal detector, mess with each other, pull on the ropes to block off areas, anything they could. This time, the metal detector went off on me. My pants had little metal grommets on them, which set off the metal detector. I was told that we wouldn't be able to visit that day, since the metal detector had been set off on 3 separate attempts. I lost it. I tried to contain my tears, but it was all I could do to just try and hide them. I don't know if the boys saw me bawling, but they for sure knew I was upset. I had listened to that ear piercing scream for the whole way there. The boys were going crazy. I was there to visit the very person who had made a selfless decision to give the boys a better life. She was giving me the most amazing gift that can be given, and being denied our visit after driving all that way with constant screaming was more than I could bear. I knew she was expecting us. It was too much to take. I tried to explain- between gasps; attempting to conceal my emotion- that the boys' birthmother had just signed the papers to allow me to adopt. I tried to hide my face. I must have been a mess. The staff took pity on me. I heard them discussing that it was obvious that the little metal things on my pants were setting off the metal detector, not any contraband. They discreetly allowed me in to visit. I couldn't look them in the eye when we came to visit for a long time.

Denial

(Nothing is wrong with the boys that can't be fixed with love.)

James gave the indication that he accepted the idea of adoption. He began writing his new last name on papers well before the adoption was final. He became very downhearted when he saw me write his previous last name on things, and was not satisfied with the explanation that I had to wait until it was final before I could write it on school documents. I was still under the false notion that the boys were emotionally secure and had the capacity for happiness and love at that time. I thought that by writing his new name, he was displaying positive feelings about the whole matter. I believed that he understood the situation, and was happy about it.

As "adoption day" neared, I became more optimistic (and disillusioned) about our life together as a family. We had some temper tantrums and displeasure expressed, of course, but I thought that there were times that they enjoyed our experiences together. I was wrong. I was out, camera ready, for all of our "firsts". They seemed to enjoy their first fishing trip. James caught a big fish, and Jackson was beaming right beside him in the picture. It looked like they had fun as we began our first annual family traditions together. We went to the state fair, we carved pumpkins, visited the pumpkin patch, went to football games, and they played in leaves for the first time. I would find out later that they wouldn't even remember many of these events that I had believed to be significant. The memories of these experiences were overwhelmed by the stress and fear that were constant for them at that time. At that point, I was blissfully unaware of this phenomenon and thought that we were creating our first memories together.

It was during this time that I had my first experience with Jackson's acting skills, too. I'm embarrassed to admit that I was such a fool, but must give credit where credit is due: Jackson was (and is) very convincing. He had several doctor visits for various ailments. He had his foot X-rayed because he was limping so severely that it surely was broken. He could remember to perform upon waking in the morning, screaming in agony as he attempted to put weight on his foot. He also discovered that frequent trips to the bathroom would result in a check for a urinary infection, which he had actually suffered from –once- in the past. The pleasure from the idea that he might get to urinate on my hand was great motivation to mimic the symptoms of an infection by displaying a frequent need to urinate. The first time he'd needed to pee in a cup, he was overjoyed when he got urine all over my hand. Even though I had him hold the cup himself during each subsequent visit, he seemed to hold out hope that I would forget.

Surprisingly, these visits to the doctor required no medical treatment. The doctors bought it, too, however. Never once did they doubt that Jackson was in pain, or that for some reason he was urinating frequently. He wasn't emptying his bladder fully, but he would likely grow out of the problem, I was told. *Ha. Right.* I still have to remind myself that he probably isn't really wounded when the broken leg appears again. My only worry is that someday, he really will have a broken limb. He has cried wolf too many times, and although I'm proud of his convincing acting skills, the uncanny ability to appear to be truly wounded may be likely to delay treatment for an actual physical injury one of these days.

During the first several months, we were getting along reasonably well. I was aware that the boys had some issues, but was still under the blissful misconception that stability and love would fix everything. I was under so much stress over everything, I would have missed the signs anyway. Jackson would allow himself to be picked up, not comforted, but incidental touches were tolerated. He still screamed in the car, and was incredibly demanding, but I figured he was just a 3 year old boy who was adjusting to a whole new life. I could handle that. James had some odd behaviors, but nothing that was extreme, and there didn't seem to be any connections among the assortment of odd behaviors. He was just a little different, and I felt as though I should accept him as he was. So what if he was a little weird? He was doing well in school, and everyone I knew was telling me how much happier he seemed. The adoption process moved along very rapidly. We had to do a lot of paperwork, run an ad in the newspaper looking for the birthfather, get lots of papers signed by the birthmother, still incarcerated, and have a home study done. All the while, we were still fighting in court over the protection order against the former grandmother. The home study was easier than anticipated, but the weekend before the adoption hearing was a nightmare. I had been taking the boys to the local high school football games. I'd always gone to the games before, and saw no reason to stop. My sister's kids play in the band, too, so watching them was just part of life for us.

The game that night was against a rival in a nearby town, but we planned to attend anyway. I had my sister's girls with me, and the boys. We went out to eat, but that was before my boys actually ate when we were at restaurants, so it was more of a half-hearted attempt to get them to stay in one place while everyone else ate. I got a call from the home study social worker as we were leaving the restaurant. She said that one of the letters of recommendation that she needed to have to complete the home study had not come in. I was actually in the town where she lived, but to obtain a sealed copy of the letter, I had to go back to the town where I work- about 30 minutes away. Thankfully the girls were able to be enough of a distraction that Jackson didn't make the car ride intolerable.

There was a storm delaying the football game, so we drove through the storm, back to work, got a copy of the letter from the lady who wrote it, and went back over. The social worker wasn't going to be home that evening, so it wouldn't matter if we dropped it off before or after the game. The game had started before we could get there, and given that it was a rival game, seats were limited. No storm delay would keep our die-hard fans away. We had to go to the game before the seats my parents were trying to save were gone. We managed to get there, but I'm sure that my dad was very nervous. He didn't like to have to save seats when there were so many people trying to cram into the bleachers. I was anxious and distracted the whole time, even though it was "the big game". I just wanted to get through it, and get the letter in the lady's mailbox. I indulged the boys to keep them quiet, despite my typical requirement that a good meal was to be eaten *before* treats. They had candy. They had popcorn. They had gum. They had pop. They were quiet. I got what I asked for (quiet, seemingly obedient children), but I paid for it later.

I used the GPS to find the lady's home after the game. New roads had been made since my GPS was updated, so we accidently took the long route. It must have been about 11:00 at night by this time. I found the house, put the letter in the box, and started for my sister's house to drop the girls back off. About 10 minutes into our 30 minute drive, the candy, gum (swallowed, of course- he was 3 and I was not saying "no"), pop, and popcorn finally caught up with Jackson. He got sick. It had already been a long night, and this was only the beginning. He managed to only make a mess in his car seat, thankfully, although I was really thinking that it would have been much easier to clean up if he'd still been in that booster seat. He got sick again in the night, and, as usual, could not be comforted. He didn't even tell me that he threw up in bed. I was really glad that I was using the camera as a baby monitor. I was able to hear him and see that he wasn't sleeping, so I went to check on him. I can't believe that he would have stayed in that mess rather than tell me, but he would have. I got him set with clean sheets, and he went back to sleep. He recovered the next day, with no signs of illness at all. I was having doubts about my parental abilities, wondering if I was even fit to be a parent. I had allowed Jackson to eat all of those foods, despite not eating supper well. I had driven all over, even through a storm, and had kept them out extremely late. I was beating myself up about it, but couldn't dwell on my insecurities too much, as there were other more pressing issues.

We went to visit the birthmother on Saturday (always a joyous event) and we had to go back to that other town to pick up the completed home study on Sunday, the day before the hearing. I was extremely nervous through the whole process, but that weekend before the hearing was the worst. We got through all of it, but I can say for certain that the few months leading up to the adoption were just a blur. The adoption hearing went fine, although I was beginning to get worried during the hearing when the judge stated that he didn't feel as if we had done enough to find the birthfather. The adoption was granted, however, and I thought that everything would finally settle down.

It was picture day at work, and I had kept James out of school. My sister's kids were there, and my parents, for the celebration. The boys got their first real gifts. I gave James a bike, and Jackson a trike. We had a cake, and I gave them a T-shirt with the mascot of our family's favorite college team. James had been asking for one. They were given gifts from my parents and sister's family, too. My sister gave me some flowers, which made it real for me. I was a mother. They seemed happy, and anyone watching would have undoubtedly agreed that they appeared content. It was still hard to take it all in, and I was overwhelmed. It very well may have been one of our last moments of peaceful ignorance.

Time, circumstance, and my lack of knowledge and understanding would all contribute to the seemingly sudden appearance of severe problems. My misguided attempts to ease the boys into our new life together, while encouraging them to hold onto their past lives was the first big mistake I made as their mother. I accepted the boys as my own without hesitation. I had no trouble loving them. The next year would test my strength, and my judgment more than ever before. My enthusiasm may have been tested and was hard to find at times, and to refer to my judgment as poor is giving me more credit than I deserve. I did more things wrong than I did right, and it took me way too long to figure that out. No matter how many times I tell myself that it was the best I could do at the time, I still struggle with forgiving myself for my actions. My emotions had been put through the ringer, and I found it hard to stay positive and act as I should. Other times, I actually thought I was doing the right thing, while in reality, I was further damaging my already wounded children.

Mistakes That Can't Be Erased

I began that first night as a mother by making one of the statements that I regret the most. I desperately hope it didn't cause James to feel rejected and delay our relationship from developing, but I cannot clear that worry from my thoughts. That night, when I went to tuck him in, I said "Good night, my son." He didn't say anything until I was leaving the room. Then he said, "Good night, Mommy". I didn't know what to say. I should have left it at that. I shouldn't have responded the way I did. At that point, I was feeling an awful lot of gratitude to the birthmother in all of this, and thought (well, not thought... knew-it was very plain to see) that James felt an enormous sense of loyalty for her. Rather than let it go, and be smart enough to let him claim me as his mother, I was stupid. I didn't want to make him feel like he had to replace his first mom- I wanted him to feel like he had gained one. I said "You don't have to call me that, if you don't want to. That can still be the name for your first mom." I said, "Maybe we can come up with a special name for me." I immediately regretted it. My initial thought was that I was helping him to deal with this difficult situation, but when the words were spoken, I realized that it didn't sound the way I had expected. Although my intent was to make sure he didn't feel like I had completely replaced his first mom, that is probably what I should have done. It was a confusing time, and at that point, I still believed that the birthmother would be a part of their lives. I didn't realize that she also contributed significantly to the trauma that they experienced. I was so wrong, and so confused about what was really going on. I really hope that he didn't take that as another rejection, but I don't know how he couldn't have. I guess it just adds to my long list of mistakes that I wish I could have prevented. Regardless, with the adoption being final, I felt an overwhelming sense of relief. It was over. I really thought it was. I didn't know that it was actually just the beginning.

The Truth Begins to Surface

Much to my distress, I had to leave the boys for several days right after the adoption was final. They were to stay with my sister, which wasn't too much of a big deal, as they had stayed there before they were mine, and they saw my sister every day, too. Our center had been provided a grant that allowed for my mom and me to go to Atlanta for an early childhood conference. The plans were made before the process for guardianship had been started. I didn't want to leave them, but figured it was the last trip I'd go on for a long time, and was obligated anyway. I probably needed the break away from everything, but it wasn't exactly the most relaxing time. I called every day. I thought about them and our new life all of the time. My mom was kind enough to be a wonderful listener as I unloaded my hopes, dreams, fears, and random thoughts. When we returned, I couldn't get to the boys fast enough.

Then came the disappointment. They didn't want to come. James was especially opposed to going back home with me. I was hurt, but tried to blow it off. I tried to tell myself that they were just having fun there because my sister's kids were around. Novelty. My thoughts were bouncing all over the place: "Why wouldn't they want to come home to see what I brought for them?" "They were just having too much fun playing with kids-there aren't cousins around all of the time." "Didn't they want to come home to their own beds?" "Don't they even care about me?" "They really like playing the video games- I'm sure they just wanted to keep playing on the kids' tablets." "My sister lets them do things that I don't- it was just like a vacation that they didn't want to end." I wanted to rationalize their behavior, but I still felt disappointed. I knew that it hadn't been very long that we'd been together, but I had hoped that they would want me. I wanted to be missed, but they were not capable at that time of holding on to anything. It was just another home- which didn't have the same definition to them. Home was simply a place to stay- not something associated with safety, security, and comfort. I wasn't meaningful, either- or at least they didn't want me to feel like I might be. I couldn't help but be disappointed driving them home that day. I'd expected them to have all sorts of things to tell me when I picked them up. Instead, the backseat was full of cries and pouting.

I was hurt, but I was still trying to justify the boys' behavior by reminding myself that this was all still new. I also had nothing to compare the behavior to. Our situation was different. I was concerned, but kept my sense of positivity. I just tried harder to be the mother I wanted to be for them. I thought that by providing the boys with love and understanding, they'd be just fine. I thought that I could get them to like me by being a good mother. I was still happy. I was still optimistic. I didn't completely understand what was going on, and I had no idea about the way our first year as a family would turn out. I thought things would only get better. I didn't know that once these issues started to grow, they couldn't be overlooked. It didn't happen all at once, however. I still had a great sense of pride in my new role of motherhood, which kept me looking to the future with eagerness and excitement.

Thanksgiving came, and I introduced my children to the extended family. Most everyone received my children with open arms. My sister-in-law had voiced her opinion to others earlier, so I knew that she wasn't coming on to the idea as easily. She thought that I should have consulted others in the family prior to the decision to adopt. I guess I should have asked her to inform me if she plans to conceive another child. I did not. I was a little offended by the attitude towards the whole matter, but I tried to avoid any conflict. She didn't necessarily treat my children poorly, but had an obvious favorite. I may have been a bit negative in my perception anyway, given my knowledge of her disapproval of the situation. I think she also disliked that we were living with my parents at that point. It wasn't much different than her living in a home provided by her grandparents, 2 blocks away from her parents, in my opinion. Regardless, almost everyone looked kindly upon our new family, and welcomed my sons with open arms. The boys were overwhelmed at Thanksgiving, but all of the kids were acting up anyway. Their behavior was not too crazy- they were wild, but no more so than the rest of the cousins.

It's not over...

Even though the adoption was final, the former grandmother wasn't going to just let things go. The protection order hearing was continued until after the adoption because our attorney had taken a long vacation. I thought the outcome of the hearing would be fine, but it only was partially in our favor. I didn't get the full protection order, but the former grandmother was given oral instructions to stay away from me and the boys, and not to contact us at all. The attorney suggested that we order transcripts from that hearing to prove that the judge had given her admonishments. We did, and it was a worthwhile endeavor, I suppose. Less than a week after the hearing, she showed up at our Christmas program for our center. Those without knowledge of the former grandmother's past attendance record for performances might get the idea that I was going out of my way just to keep the boys from her, when all she wanted to do was attend performances, as she had likely done before. Before, however, there was not this determination to attend every event. When I went to obtain the kindergarten report card for James from the year prior, on it was the message "We missed seeing James at the Christmas program, he'd worked so hard for it." Now, here she was, attempting to appear to be this doting grandmother, when in reality, the "grandmother" role hadn't ever existed.

I emailed our attorney, telling him what she had done, and the $75.00 response was "That's why the transcripts are a good idea." I didn't really appreciate the cost for that response, since I thought we had paid enough. I thought it over and decided that it wasn't worth it to pursue anything further. Although the boys saw her in the front row taking pictures, there was no interaction. She did, however, try to go backstage to approach them, but we had taken care to get them to a safe place. The lip-licking and face wiping reappeared with a vengeance, but she didn't seek them out again, at least for a few months. We began our lives together, not really knowing how things would go from that point.

Real Problems

I was sharing my parenting stories with others, and kept getting the "all kids do that" response. I was doubting my gut feeling that that something was really wrong with my children, since no one else seemed to think so. I could tell that others questioned the significance of the problems I described. I tried to go along with the idea that the boys were just fine. We went on, and my concerns grew. One event was especially troubling to me. Their birthmother had signed us up for a charity program through a local church. It was for children with incarcerated parents. I felt kind of strange taking part in it, but had agreed to it before the adoption process started, and thought it might be good for the boys to see other kids in similar situations- being cared for by people other than their birthparents. I had a really hard time even figuring out what to say to the volunteers to say what kids needed when they called to ask for sizes and suggestions. I felt like I was taking away from kids that might be in worse situations. At that time, although I didn't have a lot of money to spare, we were not struggling too much. The boys had appropriate clothing, they had what they needed, and a bit more. I hadn't bought too many toys, but we were all doing just fine. We were still living with my parents, and trying to pay off loans.

The day of the event was freezing. The wind chill was well below zero. I bundled them up in their sweaters, long underwear (which they hadn't ever seen before), coats and gloves. I dressed them pretty nicely- not fancy, but they looked decent and festive in solid red and green sweaters. I had gone over with them the appropriate behavior and social expectations. I made sure that they knew to say "thank you", and explained that even if they didn't think they liked the gift, they should be sure to tell the people that they appreciated it.

The people hosting the event were incredibly welcoming and pleasant. They saw to it that the kids had things to do, coloring materials and things like a train set to play with. Jackson really liked that. There were some foster families, some grandparents with grandchildren, and a few other relatives with kids. The families were kind and respectful. Some made a little bit of conversation, but not too much. The volunteers were very conscientious in seeing that every person was spoken to. It was really nice. A meal was offered, and they helped me and the boys go through the food line at the same time, carrying plates and drinks. They made conversation while at the table, as well. I was uncomfortable, but without their welcoming attitude and effort to make everyone at ease, it would have been extremely difficult. They went out of their way to make everyone feel good. It was a pleasant atmosphere.

It was not a chaotic event, initially. All of the children were pretty well-mannered, the families polite, everything was going well. I felt a little guilty having my kids well-dressed, though. The boys had on several layers and well-fitting coats. Many of the kids wore ill-fitting clothing and wore only T-shirts and thin pants on that frigid day. They truly needed the clothing being provided to them. My boys had experienced wearing inappropriate clothing only a few months before, but were now taken care of. It made me grateful that they were now taken care of, but it was sad to see other kids that were still in a similar situation to what my boys had been in. I wish that the feeling of guilt was the worst that came from that event, but it wasn't.

They gave each child a bible, for which I was very appreciative. I had been wanting to give the boys one. They have treasured their bibles, too. Then came the time to distribute gifts. They brought the presents to our table. Two people carried two gifts each and set them on the table. I saw the name on the top of each stack, and handed each child their gifts. James and Jackson began to open very quickly. It started out fine. James was thrilled with what he opened, which happened to be the toys. Jackson saw the clothing, and immediately went to the next box. When he saw that it contained clothing as well, his face began to prepare for the fire engine wail that was inevitably coming. I immediately tried to console him, and figure out what was going on. I then realized that James had opened two boxes of toys. The bottom boxes were mixed up. Although one box on top said "Jackson" and one said "James"- the ones on the bottom were for the other child. Jackson had opened the clothes boxes, and James the toys.

Once I realized it, I thought that after I got it straightened out with Jackson, we'd be fine. I took the box James was opening, and said "Hang on a minute, I need to see if this one is for Jackson". Jackson quit crying, and awaited his gift. Then James began screaming. Not just a little, either. I tried to explain that one box was his, and one was Jackson's. I handed him the box that contained clothing in his size. He was screaming, flailing, stomping, and running up on Jackson as if he were a charging bull. He'd pace around, and then repeat the charge. I was mortified. I am sure that my face was as red as the festive sweater I had James wearing. I looked around, and pointed out to him all of the grateful children, happy with their gifts. I sat him down on a chair, and got right at his eye level. I spoke quickly and tried to come up with something that would get him to stop. I started begging. I squeezed his legs as I spoke, trying to get his attention. That only caused him to scream louder as if I had mortally wounded him. He was gasping and screaming in long, drawn out cries, gasping and screaming again. No words. I then realized that we needed to get out of there. Jackson was a bit of a mess, confused and wanting to hide, but he was actually handling things very well, considering. I told him that he would get his toys, but that James was being very naughty and that I needed him to help me.

He ran to hide a time or two, but mostly he was helpful. It was not going to be easy to get out of there with the gifts, our heavy coats (for which I had been so grateful just moments before), and two kids, one screaming his fool head off. I searched out a trash can and quickly put our paper trash in. I asked Jackson to carry the bibles, and although he initially said no, the look on my face must have been desperate. He complied. I thought we were going to make it out of there OK, but then I realized that James was not going to walk out on his own. We started out without him, but he wouldn't come. The kind folks there tried to talk with him, and I made a quick, probably unintelligible, attempt to explain what had happened. They offered to help with our things, which I should have taken them up on, but I just wanted to get out of that place with as few people taking obvious notice as possible. I put the gifts in one box, added the bibles from Jackson's hands, and handed the too-large box to him. He gave me a funny look, but I told him how big he was to be such a great helper. I said "Look how strong you are!" I picked up James and prodded Jackson along, out of the room to get our coats. I stuffed the hats and gloves into the box, put the coat on Jackson, and threw the coat over James as I hauled him out of there, with one hand on the box to make sure Jackson didn't drop it. I shoved James in the car, buckled him, and drove off, completely shaken with embarrassment and disappointment. I didn't know what to say or do. Those people had been so kind, and I felt as if we had ruined their wonderful event.

James went from screaming without words to a new chant-something like "I want my toys". I hollered back at him- telling him how ungrateful and hurtful he was. I made it clear that I thought that he should care about his little brother, too. I asked him why he would want Jackson to miss out on toys. I told him how the clothes intended for him wouldn't even fit Jackson. I, without realizing the pointlessness of my lecture, started many statements with the words "How would you feel..." How would he feel? I was asking a child without the ability to label even his own emotions, to have sympathetic feelings for others. I was truly asking the impossible. I didn't know that my statements were relevant only for children with healthy emotional regulation, but I *was* aware that nothing I was saying was working. He was still in his selfish mode, which wouldn't be remedied for years to come.

I needed to talk to someone. I didn't exactly know what I was going to say, but I needed someone to help me make sense of this disaster of an event. I called my mother, but she couldn't be reached. I called my sister and the story was received with shock and giggles. I finally got my mother, but I knew that no matter how much I tried to describe the events of the day, no one could possibly understand the pure misery during and after that experience. I couldn't believe that James could be so selfish, and I was so upset that the people had been so kind, and we appeared so ungrateful.

I told James that he needed to figure out how to explain what he was thinking, adding to my impossible requests. I was probably very frightening to him, but he didn't change his behavior, or even pretend to change his perception. He thought that "It wasn't fair" and that "the toys were his". After well over 2 hours of listening to the screaming, I lost any semblance of patience that I once had. He said something that sent me over the edge. I was making rice, and when his statement asserting his need for the toys came through the bedroom door- I couldn't take it anymore. I can't even remember the exact words, but it was something that implied that he was entitled to those toys, and there wasn't a whine in his voice at all. There was some anger, and an assertion of power. He was insisting that he *was* going to have all the toys. I went into the bedroom, and said that I never wanted to hear those words come out of his mouth again. His response was not desirable. I don't know what he could have said that would have made the situation less difficult, but the words he chose were certainly not the best ones. It was a response that only reiterated his belief that all the toys were his, and that he was the one being wronged. I turned him over and spanked him. He couldn't have been physically pained too much, with all of those layers on, but anyone within miles wouldn't have been able to tell that from his response. He screamed and retreated into the corner.

I felt guilt, hopelessness, shame, anger, sadness, fear, and confusion all at the same time. What had I done? Here I was, trying to teach him to be compassionate, and I had resorted to spanking to try and get the message across. I stormed back to the kitchen, my mind a swirling mess of thoughts, only to be brought back to reality to find the rice scorching. I wanted to cry. I don't think that I made all the right choices that day, but I would like to think that anyone in that situation would struggle to do so, too. Experience has strengthened my ability to make better choices now, but I still have trouble knowing what to do. Discovering and strengthening the will to keep emotions from contributing to chaos was a difficult, yet vital task. I don't think anyone can prepare themselves for coping with these unforeseen problems. Only experiencing them firsthand gives a person the opportunity and desire to strive to do better when the next time comes around.

There were many events that made me see how troubled the boys were, but I didn't fully grasp the extent of the problems for quite some time.

Christmas was a bit overwhelming, and there were issues of jealousy and selfishness, but it didn't go as badly as I thought it could have, aside from Christmas morning. Before Christmas came, James went around telling everybody it was his "first Christmas". We decorated the tree, made cookies, had an advent calendar- all new and exciting things for the boys. They were pretty much spoiled that Christmas anyway, because they had so little to start with. They had plenty of clothes to unwrap, some toys, and other things that I thought all kids needed. Christmas morning was one of those events that brought surprise, but not in the positive way I had imagined.

It made me more certain in my belief that my sons were not like most kids. They didn't wake up early, for starters. I had to wake them up because it was time for breakfast, and we had company coming. I had gotten them coordinating pajamas, ready for their "first Christmas" photographs. I was so excited! Our family tradition is to open gifts from each other on Christmas Eve, so Santa was the big thing for Christmas Day anyway, other than celebrating and eating with extended family. They waddled, half-asleep, into the living room, and sat down right in front of the gifts. At first, I thought that maybe they were just really tired. The day before had been quite busy and overwhelming. I soon realized that they were awake, but appeared oblivious to the gifts surrounding them. They looked, but didn't show any emotion. The pictures I took were horrible. I am glad I had the presence of mind not to delete them, so I can remember and look back at how things once were. I almost deleted them on the spot. They are terrible pictures. They are sitting there, surrounded by gifts, looking miserable.

Even when they began to open gifts and empty the stockings, there was little excitement. There were 2 new sleds sitting there, along with the other toys and gifts, but it was as if they really didn't see them. I was awfully disappointed. I had talked with a friend before about being so excited that my first Christmas as a mother I would get to see the kids really excited and happy. Most first time mothers have infants. I was pleased at the thought of being able to enjoy Christmas with my kids as a first time mom. I had made sure that Santa brought fun things, I'd gone all out with the cookies, milk, and carrots for the reindeer. I was stunned when they looked so solemn. I expected to see their little faces full of delight. I never really understood the whole situation, but I once read a book written by someone with a child from a traumatic background, and was brought to tears as the same experience was described.

The boys eventually came around, sort of, and James read the letter from Santa, explaining their big gift from Santa. "Santa" brought money for us to take a weekend trip. We were going to a city that was a little over 2 hours away. We were to go to Build-A-Bear so they could have their very own teddy bears, and to one of those themed restaurants- this was a dinosaur one. My sister joined us for part of the trip, and we all had a good time, surprisingly. It was bitter cold, and rather than stay at the outdoor sights by the restaurant, we went home. There were minor difficulties- odd behavior was typical for us at that time. Nothing noteworthy, though. It was nice. We really hadn't done much until then with enjoyment as the purpose. We'd gone places and done things, but usually on the way to other obligations. We only stayed one night, but it went well. We still did a visit with the birthmother that weekend, but I can't recall it being any more difficult than it usually was. We (my sister's family and us) had adjacent rooms at the hotel, and my sister told me later that my brother-in-law questioned whether they should check on us, on account of the screaming. It was never pleasant or easy when the boys were involved, but it could have been worse. The other factor contributing to a better trip was that the boys had been given tablets by my parents for Christmas. The car ride was much nicer. It was odd to me, though, that they preferred watching videos to playing games at that time. As far as gifts, I realized very quickly that the boys had a strong aversion to anything *I* gave them. They didn't mention any of the gifts that I had given them when people asked what they got for Christmas. They chose to open the gifts that had been sent through a charity "from" their birthmother first. They recalled each gift from everyone else, but could never mention mine. They didn't even play with what I got for them. I was hurt, but the reassurance from everyone else that it was fine kept making me think that I was just being overly sensitive and crazy.

What is Normal?

I kept trying to do the "normal" things with the boys, but we couldn't do normal. We were invited to the neighbor's birthday party (oddly enough, we were not invited the following year-can't imagine why). It was a bowling party. First time for everything (last time for us for a while). I told the boys that the ball was heavy, so they needed to be careful and not drop it on their feet. We hadn't been in there 2 minutes, and James had already picked up a ball way too heavy for him and dropped it on his foot. There were no major wounds from the accident, but he screamed dramatically. They did not know how to take turns, which makes a game like bowling extremely challenging. Jackson, still 3 at this time, refused to allow me to help him. I was trying to pick the ball up for him, to avoid having his hand trapped in the ball-return belt, all the while warning him that his fingers were going to get smashed when the ball came up, and hit the other ones. I'm sure you can guess what happened. His smashed fingers were red and shaking as he gave out some of his best screams. I insisted then that I get the ball, and carry it out so he could roll it. He was trying to push me out of the way, and grab the ball from my hands. I was looking like a big fool. I finally let him carry the ball, but then was terrified as he kept taking his hand off of the ball to push me away. It was most

76

unpleasant to be having this lovely interaction with my son in front of so many families I knew and worked with.

James was just acting crazy. He was climbing on the seats, jumping off of them, and playing with the keyboard that controls the scoring screen. I had asked him several times to just leave it alone. They spilled drinks, and ate about 4 pieces of pizza each, even though I had just fed them before the party. When it was time for cake, the birthday boy's mom was passing out the cake. She had chocolate and white cupcakes. She went around the table offering the choices for the cupcakes, only to be requested for ice cream by my rude 6 year old. I wish that was the end of it, but it wasn't. There were a bunch of party favors. Rubber bouncy balls, and these little ice cream cone foam ball shooters. James went right for the parents with the ice cream shooter. Parents he didn't even know. He ended up wrestling on the floor with other kids, and climbing atop a cement wall in the center of the bowling alley. I wanted to crawl in a hole. I finally said that we had to be somewhere, and left. On the way out the door, James realized that his ice cream cone shooter was broken, so he responded immediately with moaning wails. Jackson, at nearly the same time, had bounced that stupid ball, only to have it ricochet off of the wall and bounce down a lane. I had to carry him out of there screaming. James moved his feet about a half an inch at a time as we left there, just to be sure that as many people as possible could hear him.

There were other incidents during this time that opened my eyes to the major problems we were facing. James was still refusing to use the bathroom, and would soil his pants frequently. I could see him trying not to go, and I would request that he use the bathroom. After he had lied too many times about his need to use the bathroom, my frequent requests to "try" began to incite screaming fits. It was most unpleasant. I had been upset with him over the messy pants for a while, but then realized that he really wasn't intending to do it. I had him clean out his underwear, so his favorite trick was to wait until it was time for a bath to tell me that his underwear was dirty. He threw spectacular fits the first few times he had to do it, but then it became just an everyday task. I would buy a toy equivalent in price for Jackson when I had to buy new underwear after too many had been discarded because it was too much of a mess to clean, or if we were not at home when I discovered that he needed to change. This didn't have much impact on his toileting habits. He was very much matter-of-fact about it. I carried extra underwear for my 6 year old, but never needed any for my 3 year old. It was an odd situation. I was trying very hard not to make it a big deal, but it was hard not to be upset when I saw him holding his body awkwardly and still refusing to go to the bathroom when I told him to. I don't believe he had actually gone to use the bathroom on his own since I had gotten him, at that point. It was really frustrating. One day, after many days of messy pants, I had a revelation. I remembered that one child in my class a year or two before had the same problem. A child adopted from foster care. The similarity in that one behavior opened my eyes. I began to see the other similarities and quirky behaviors. I figured there was something significant about that odd likeness in the two boys, but couldn't find any other connection besides the fact that they were adopted. I tried to tell myself that this was just something that these kids must go through. Long-term issues weren't really on my mind at that point.

The mistakes I made were adding up during this time. I continued to sign James up for sports, I was still bringing them to see their birthmother (despite their horrid behavior there), I occasionally yelled and spanked- never physically causing injury, but inflicting harm anyway. I was becoming less and less patient. I failed to see how everything I did was so massively impacting the boys' entire being. I remember once while I was working during the weekend in my classroom, doing some paperwork. These hard plastic footballs from a fast food restaurant were the toys of choice at the moment for the boys. They were not playing with them as intended (there was a little plastic guy with an arm to attach the football to). The balls were flying all over the room, and were knocking things over. I warned the boys that they needed to stop. Jackson threw one that bounced on the table where I was working. I unintentionally encouraged an escalation of behavior by saying "Stop", and "If that hits me, or comes near me again, I'm going to throw it away."

Those might not have been the best choice of words, but I still hadn't learned that these kids were going to test every limit I set. I also had no idea that those particular words would strike a nerve with James. It took a matter of seconds before Jackson chucked that ball at me. That hard plastic ball made contact with the top of my head just as I sat down and leaned over the table attempting to resume my work. A professional marksman couldn't have had better aim. I took the ball (one of many we had at the time, as we had fast food on home football game nights through the fall) and put it in the trash. Jackson started crying, but James began wandering around. He was upset, but I didn't understand his language of behavior at the time. He went to retrieve the ball from the trash. I told him to leave it. I remember pointing out that I was happy that he finally seemed to care about his brother, but that I had warned them, and reminded him that we had many more of those footballs. He threw a little bit of a fit, and then recovered, which was odd for him. Fits from him were measured in hours, not minutes. He paced the classroom, and got out a dry-erase board and marker. He wrote the words "I hate you" on it.

I was not just hurt by this statement, I was mad. I couldn't figure out why this was upsetting him so much. He didn't seem to care about anything. He never showed compassion for his brother, he didn't have any favorite toys, he damaged things right and left. Why was throwing away this little thing so significant to him? I tried to talk with him, but he threw the board at me. I had gotten very little work done, because the boys couldn't stay out of trouble for any amount of time, my head hurt from that stupid football, a lap board had been hurled in my direction. I had one son writing that he hated me, and another throwing his shoes at the ceiling and windows, making the blinds a mess. I was no longer able to keep my patience. It was one of the only times I spanked him with much chance of him being able to feel any sensation of physical pain. I regret it, of course. I don't even know exactly why I did it, aside from the fact that I was simply being worn down. My ability to think clearly was gone. I felt hurt. I felt angry that I had lost control. I was upset that James had expressed that he hated me, and I was even more upset with myself due to the way I had responded. After being told "I hate you", I guess I simply gave him a reason to do just that. I did a lot of stupid things.

James later shared with me that "Nana" had once thrown away something of his that he really liked. I admit, regretfully, that I was skeptical of his story at the beginning. I hadn't found anything that he seemed to care about. It was hard to believe that he might have actually cared about anything. He was descriptive in his story, and told me that it was a toy snake. I asked why she did it. He said that he was bad. I assumed, of course, that he had been doing something hurtful with it, or maybe left it out and when it was should have been put away. I was remembering the incident in the therapist's office when I had been slapped with the wet snake, thinking maybe "Nana" could have been justified if something like that had happened. He said he hadn't been hitting anyone with it, but that he was bad and she went to the toy box and found the snake. Then she went to the trashcan and threw it away. He confided that he screamed and went to get it out, but she spanked him and put him in the corner and took out the trash.

After he told the whole story, I believed him. I still do. I tried to explain, to no avail, that one of the countless little footballs being thrown away after repeatedly hitting me was different than the situation he described. He wouldn't even pretend to see a difference. Something was being thrown away. That's all that mattered. I replayed this scene from his description in my head, again and again. Why would anyone seek out a child's favorite toy with the purpose to get rid of it and cause him pain? She was evil, and I was angry. I was upset that I had done something to allow James to compare me to her. This only added to the whirlwind of emotions that was my constant state. I was stressed, angry, frustrated, and completely overwhelmed. The plunk on the head from that plastic football was minor compared to the constant behavior problems and emotional stress from both boys. I wasn't dealing well. Knowing how hurt they actually were was bittersweet.

Realizing that they were so hurt helped me to understand their behavior in one way, but built up these strong feelings of resentment and hatred toward their abusers. This was also unhealthy, and contributed to my stress. The boys' behavior was so challenging that being under such stress made it difficult, if not impossible, to display the patience and understanding they needed. I was exhausted. They were constantly fighting; they couldn't be left alone for a second. They would damage things or hurt each other. Mealtimes were torture. James wouldn't try anything, and refused to eat many foods. Nothing fast or easy would appeal to him. No peanut butter and jelly sandwiches, no grilled cheese, no hot dogs, no chicken nuggets, no macaroni and cheese, few vegetables, and fewer fruits. It was a difficult job trying to get him to eat. Jackson would follow his big brother's example, too. The screaming fits at home were becoming more frequent and were lasting a really long time. I knew my dad was reaching his limit. Children are sometimes referred to as "little monsters", but at that point, I'm not entirely sure which of us could be considered the biggest monster. I feel like *I* turned into a monster at that point. I was desperate to get the behavior changed, and I gave the appearance of being a harsh, uncaring mother.

It looked as if the kids couldn't do anything right in my eyes, which was nearly the case. The reality was that their behavior created the difficulty, and they were extraordinarily skilled in causing emotional pain. It was directed at me, and I couldn't figure out how to handle it. I strongly disagree with blaming children for the wrongdoing of adults. I, however, was not strong enough at that time to fully understand the relationship (or lack thereof) the boys had worked very hard to create. I was a puppet. If you have not experienced this type of relationship firsthand, you may feel as if I am exaggerating, or maybe have a sense of doubt that children could have that much control over an adult. I admit without hesitation that I once had that same belief. That was before I really knew my children. I never caused significant physical harm to the boys. I spanked sometimes, but not to the point of causing lasting pain. I think I was most harmful when I didn't spank them, actually. Yelling really upset them, and on occasion, I would pick them up more forcefully than I like to admit, and I'm quite sure it was scary, as I was likely speaking through clenched teeth. I was also beginning to cover their mouths when they would start to scream, as I felt that my parents should not have to put up with that in their home that they were so kind to share with us. I would try to quiet the screams while in places like hotel rooms, as well.

Hotel stays were still a new concept. They became very unsettled, and I remember one of our first hotel stays very well. Jackson was a mess. It was late in the evening, and he had absolutely no semblance of self-control. I didn't have much at that point, either. He was screaming because it was time for bed, and I had said that he couldn't have a can of pop. I knew that everyone in the hotel could hear him. I spanked him- his pull-up clad bottom and fleece-lined athletic pants made an impressive sound, but he couldn't have possibly felt physical pain from my hand. The circumstance itself was the damaging part. James ran and hid as if I had just beaten a child to death. Jackson was still screaming that blood curdling scream, and James was in a state of panic trying to make himself disappear into the curtain. I was at a really low point. I didn't know what to do. I told James that Jackson was fine, and tried to point out that he had so much covering his bottom that I may as well have smacked him with a pillow. Jackson paused for a minute, laughed at that thought, and then remembered that he was supposed to be having a fit. His face returned to that angry state (we referred to it as the "I hate you face"), and he resumed his screaming and flailing. I decided to just go ahead and put him in the tub. I washed him- aggressively is probably the best way to describe how, (yup, mistake, after mistake, again and again) and got him into bed. Then it was time to figure out how to get James under control and into bed.

These incidents were the norm for us at that time. There wasn't a day that went by that we didn't have a story to tell. I felt overwhelmed and deflated. I am still so disappointed in myself when I remember these occasions. I am disgusted with the person I had become. I was doing everything I could to help the boys, but I was not doing as well as they needed me to do. I was trying to keep my patience, but I was struggling every minute of every day. The boys knew it, and almost seemed to prey upon my weaknesses. They would act worse when I was most needing them to behave, and when it would embarrass me the most. James was a master of throwing fits that would last hours. We called them "dying cow fits", because the moaning sound he could make tirelessly for hours resembled that of a dying cow. It was horrid. The worst part was after the fit, though. He would turn it off and appear happy and content quite easily. I would listen to the fit for hours. I would try to calm him, I would beg, I would give explanations, options, loving gestures, only to be shut down and pushed away. Then, after I was exhausted from the length of the fit and the attempts to help him, he would suddenly turn it off- usually as another person was coming into the vicinity. I was a wreck, yet he was being personable and charming with whomever he could find. It might be when my parents returned from an outing, or when someone came to visit, or as we arrived at work or school. I felt completely drained and beat, but he could turn on the joyfulness and calm. I am sure I looked like a fool. Other people's looks asked, "How could she be so upset with this angelic child?" Anything I said to try and explain his behavior was viewed as an exaggeration or completely false.

This went on for quite some time. I was trying to keep myself together, but I was falling apart- and it wasn't just a little at a time. I realize now, how I must have appeared to everyone else, but again, I don't honestly know what I could have done differently at that time. We were supposed to be this wonderful family. I got so tired of hearing people say what a wonderful thing they thought I had done. It made me feel physically ill. I was ashamed of myself. I felt like I should have been doing better. I didn't really want everyone to know how hard things really were, but I felt deceitful while I was being told what a great thing that I was doing. We were miserable, but everyone else saw only the façade.

The boys were incapable of having fun, which made me feel like a failure. They put on a great show for everyone else, with me as the fool. I was unable to please them in any way, shape, or form, and every interaction was negative. I accept responsibility for my part in that, but also realize that their life circumstances created the need for them to create the chaos. Their actions, while seemingly intentional, were simply a part of the healing process. It was a start. Pushing me away was a test. They needed to know

84

that I was still going to stay with them. I wasn't going to withhold love as leverage. They were going to be loved, regardless of their behavior. I guess I passed the course (so far), but I didn't do so well on many of those tests. I wish I had known then the purpose behind those difficult behaviors. It was not a time I'd like to do again, however. It was really hard to want to be a good mother, while dealing with an enormous amount of other problems. The boys' behavior was certainly a part of it, but feeling poorly about myself made everything harder. I was frustrated with myself, and knew that people perceived my interactions with the boys very critically. I probably would have viewed myself the same way if I hadn't experienced it.

The boys made things difficult, and coping was tough. They pushed every limit possible, and made it so minor requests turned into significant issues. I would end up getting after them for something seemingly minute, but it typically stemmed from an earlier issue. Others saw this as overbearing and felt that I was too hard on them. Things like taking the knives from the silverware set at the restaurant was looked upon as odd or paranoid. No one realized that they had already discovered that they could use the knife to stab and damage the table during previous restaurant visits. My mom was pretty good about it, but most of my closest family viewed me as cruel to the boys. I feel that sometimes it came to that, but usually, I had good reason for limiting the boys' access to certain things, and keeping them very close. On top of the struggle I had regarding others' perceptions, I was still dealing with the former grandmother in court.

Perception

After the former grandmother showed up at the Christmas program, I thought I would hear from her in an attempt to send the boys a card or gift. When she didn't, I thought maybe she was done. She was not. There was supposed to be a music program at James's school on Jackson's birthday. I just knew she would come. They cancelled it for snow, and I was relieved. I don't know if she intended to go or not, but that night she did some crazy stuff. She had called earlier in the week at my work to try and get my sister to arrange a time for her to meet up with me. My sister told her that we weren't interested in meeting right now. The former grandmother then posted a false negative review of our center on the business webpage, and posted a negative statement about me on a Facebook page of an acquaintance of my sister that works in the school district. It was likely seen by many people we have professional relationships with. It specifically mentioned me by name. I let it go, but was displeased about it.

When the program was rescheduled for James, I was extremely worried about "Nana" showing up. I appeared to be paranoid, as I warned the school that James was not to be approached before, during, or after the program by anyone but me. I watched the doors with terror as the people arrived to watch their children. I felt robbed of enjoying my son's performance, all because I was scared of that crazy woman showing up. I felt like maybe I was the crazy one instead, but months later, I would learn that I was justified in my concern.

Jackson's actual birthday went fairly well- I think it was easier since there was a change of plans. I had made a monkey-shaped cake for the weekend for family, and he seemed to like the gifts he received. My sister had given us tickets to the circus, which, at the time I thought was great. I still had that crazy belief that we could have fun together. The hotel was right next to the building where the circus was- so it was wonderful to just be able to walk there upon leaving. One less transition.

Upon arriving at the circus, Jackson looked frightened, but there wasn't even anything going on. I kept candy and little snacks in my purse, and even that only slightly distracted him. A small band came in to play before the circus. They played a song or two before the Star Spangled Banner. Poor Jackson thought that it was over after that, and looked miserable. Almost as a statement, and not of disappointment, just simple fact, Jackson said "Is it over?" and began to sadly, without anger, get up to leave. I told him no, and said that it hadn't even started yet. He quietly sat down, still looking worried, and not exactly believing me. The show began, and James appeared to enjoy it immensely. Jackson seemed preoccupied with it being over and having to leave. He said he didn't want to go, but he just kept thinking it was over. He finally laughed at a few performances, and smiled at a few amazing feats. I wanted them to have something to remember from the circus, and the announcers pretty much trap parents into buying those light-up toys anyway. I was only getting the small spinning toy- it was $9 or $12. James only wanted the bigger one- it was $15 or $18. Although we weren't nearly to the point of financial distress that we would come to know, I wasn't going to spend the extra money on the big one just because that's the only one he thought he wanted. I told him that he could spend some of his Christmas money on it, to make up the difference. He didn't want to do that. He didn't even want to get the smaller one, then. And so the evening went from there. We had to hunt out a restroom to allow him to do a dying cow fit without people being able see us. Actually, a more accurate reason would be so we wouldn't have to look at the people hearing and seeing us, as there was no way to silence the dying cow.

I was getting really upset. We were supposed to be having fun. I seemed to only see people with happy children (I must have been really delusional at that point, because I know that there had to have been other children at the circus having fits, too). Once we entered the restroom, he turned on screams. These *weren't* typical for James. He was sounding as if he was being beaten! Instead of the dying cow moan, he was now screaming with a sense of urgency and fear. Maybe he really did think I was going to hurt him- I don't know. I didn't really resort to spanking frequently- especially with James, and never injuriously. It seemed more like an attempt for him to get his way, but I'm not sure that the toy was the goal. He either wanted people to see how miserable I was making him, or make them think that I was hurting him. It didn't seem as if getting the toy was the true purpose. I dragged him back to the seat- actually having to carry him down the steps because he wouldn't come. He was blocking the aisle, and people were having to go down the other side of the railing to avoid him. He didn't scream at that, or flail, which was my other concern. I could see myself falling down those cement steps carrying a child too big to be carried, in front of the entire arena. He moped in his seat, and eventually turned it off, saying he wanted to get the smaller toy. The show was starting, and I said we had to wait until after. He gave a big moaning noise, and went under the seat the best he could, but surfaced with no indication of displeasure on his face when the lights went out to start the second part of the show.

Then came the act. The terrible act. There was a clown with a snow globe, and the announcer's role was to try to convince the clown to put the snow globe away. He refused, and finally, the announcer took the snow globe and threw it into a trash can. James was making unintelligible sounds and burrowing into his seat at this point. He missed the finale of the act- as the snow globe was thrown away and as the sounds of breaking glass were heard throughout the arena, it began to "snow" over the stage. Snow dropped down from the ceiling and the clown was joyous at seeing his snow globe in a spectacular way. James missed it. Throwing belongings away, just as I had started to do with that little football thing that had knocked me in the head, reminded him of a painful experience. I should have saved my breath when I tried to convince him that it wasn't the same kind of thing. I told him that I felt bad that "Nana" had thrown away his stuff, but that it wasn't the same. I didn't understand then, that the situation *was* the same to him. I should have seen these signs and picked up on how traumatic these past events were for him. I didn't necessarily try to belittle him for feeling that way, but wrong as it was, my intent was to convince him that things were fine. Nothing was fine. I had two very damaged little boys that couldn't even enjoy a circus. To top it all off, the birthday celebration only exacerbated the jealousy in James. At that time, I still couldn't figure him out. He was having fits for no apparent reason all of the time, so I didn't think that him being jealous might have been the root of the ones near Jackson's birthday. Maybe they were, but at that time, the fits were so frequent, there is no way to know.

Jackson was worse, usually. Everything caused a fit. I chalked it up to age and circumstances. He was allowing me to console him more frequently, and began to display affection but only on his terms. He would give me hugs, but he would not permit me to reciprocate. Upon waking in the night after a dream, or if he was uncomfortable (he had a bad cold once, and couldn't breathe, but wouldn't blow his nose), he would not allow me to touch him. In the night, he was the same child I brought home months ago. He was distant, and could not be touched. It was hard for me to deal with. I wanted so much for him to accept my love and allow me to be there for him. I was his mother, but to him, he had no mother. It was hard. During the day, he would make demands of me, and I would do everything I could to please him. Then it would be wrong. I really could not win. He was driving me crazy, but in all honestly, compared to James, I didn't feel that his behavior was the most troubling. I worried about Jackson, but he was extremely young, and had gone through some major life changes. Most of his behaviors were age-appropriate, it was just that he was able to demonstrate them with an increased frequency and intensity compared to most children his age. I really thought that he would come around. He had become a different child during the time I had gotten him. He went from being an untouchable child, to one that was brimming with personality. He became funny, cute, and charming- at least when he wasn't demanding, angry, and screaming.

James, on the other hand, had not really changed. He had some really odd behaviors, and many people just ignored them or laughed. Even my sister just implied he was a weird kid. And he was. He would rub his head on me like a cat constantly. He couldn't display any real emotion or affection. The hugs I was given were so tight that it was almost painful. He couldn't do anything gently. The "high-fives" he'd give to my sister's kids would leave them holding their hands in pain.

James even looked odd. He couldn't really walk with a typical gait- he would gallop. It was pretty disturbing to see him galloping around and waving his hands like fairy wings. It was similar to the flapping self-stimulating behavior of a child with

90

autism, but different in a way I can't quite describe. While on the trampoline, he wouldn't jump. He would trot flat-footed around the trampoline. He would grin a lot, act incredibly silly, and show no remorse or consideration for others. He would ask the same question again and again, even if it really didn't have an answer. He'd say "Hi" every 10 seconds. He gave the appearance to others of being happier though. He had gone from being sent out of the room and suspended in kindergarten to having better-than-average behavior in 1st grade. He reserved his fits for me, typically.

The only thing that had changed was the length of his fits (they got longer), and the frequency (multiple times per day instead of occasionally). I had signed him up for flag football, which went fair. He didn't really seem to get the game, but gave that overly silly performance displaying his pleasure with the game. He did fair at basketball, but his lack of coordination and difficulty with determination prevented him from being very successful. He never implied that he didn't enjoy it tremendously, however. Then came soccer. It was in the spring, and he loved it, to the best of my knowledge.

It was during this time that I pursued further options for help. There were too many "little things" that were becoming problematic. All in the same week, after running a toy tractor into Jackson's knee- hard- he was so pleased with himself that he laughed the most joyous laugh I had ever heard him display; he soiled his pants pretty much every day; he nearly knocked down an older lady carrying a large bag of pet food as he darted under her arms to enter a store; he'd slammed the door in the face of a friend leaving the building right behind him; He'd been so rude to the other kids during soccer practice (cutting in line, telling them that he was better, pushing them, touching them when it was their turn, taking the ball when it was someone else's turn to dribble, etc.); He had responded with "I know" when kids had told him he did well- on more than one occasion, even after I had provided him with more appropriate responses. I had gotten after him for hurting my niece and nephew before school one day (a violent hand-squeeze and high-five slap), only to have him go to school and have a better-than-average behavior report. I had sent my son to school upset and crying (without tears), only to worry about him all day and find out after school that his behavior report was better than usual.

That week was enough to send me looking for help again. The therapist we had tried at first hadn't really been helpful, and the area we live in lacks in mental health services. There is a university nearby that has a clinic that provides services as the therapists become fully licensed. I had to wait a little bit for the appointment, and by the time I got in, I had pretty much diagnosed James with Reactive Attachment Disorder myself. I really wanted the clinic to see Jackson, too, but they wanted to start with James, given his age, and since he was the primary concern I had mentioned upon scheduling the appointment. I had looked up ways to attempt to appropriately address the behaviors we were dealing with, but I hadn't been looking up specific behaviors while including the term "adoption". I finally did, and when I read what I found, I was floored. When I read the symptom list, it was as if they had been written just for James. He fit nearly every aspect of the disorder I could find. The internet searches I had done included things like "adopted child & no empathy", and "adopted child & hurtful behavior". I may have even typed in "adopted child won't stop talking", though I'm not entirely sure. It certainly was a problem, though.

When I went for the initial consult at the university, I expressed my concerns, they did all of the background stuff, and we set up the appointment. James came and acted up- the sillies were overwhelmingly present. We were going to have to pay $40 per session, and I would have to take two trips to the town 25 minutes away every week. One time for James, and once with just me. The other concern was that Jackson wouldn't be treated. The would-be therapist was kind, but didn't seem to know enough about what we were dealing with. We went through a very short evaluation, and upon leaving, James gave a great display of inappropriate behavior. He was running around the lobby as I tried to speak with the therapist about how we would proceed. He kept ringing the bell on the receptionist's desk, and running to open the screen door that would shut with a slam. Then he would return and do it again. I caught him after a couple laps, but he kicked me and ran out. Then he went to the desk again and changed the wooden block-type calendar that was on the desk. The receptionist asked him to leave it on the right date, but he didn't. Then came the bell-ringing again. I was really getting upset. I caught him again as he tried to run past, looked right at him and said "That's enough! Stop!" He proceeded to continue his game. All the while, the would-be therapist was saying "he's ok". In my opinion, he was not OK. It was not acceptable to ring the bell or change the calendar after being asked to stop. Kicking me, too, was just not something to be overlooked as being an "ok" behavior. I left the facility with only minimal hope for help from there. I was worried, too, about the continuity of treatment. Since it was a teaching clinic, I knew that the student therapist wouldn't be there forever. I was worried about having to go through the whole process of finding someone else when that person left.

I kept looking for someone else to help us, and found a place that looked more promising. It was 2 hours away, however. I didn't hesitate too much, but the distance was a deterring factor. I requested information, and decided to go for it. I could not find anyone near us with the credentials for treating RAD. The thought of my son becoming a serial killer was motivation enough to find a qualified, experienced therapist, no matter the distance or inconvenience. I couldn't risk using a student therapist, who may or may not have been able to help, when my son was displaying so evidently the symptoms of such a serious disorder. Jackson could also be seen right away. I will never regret that choice. Anyway, through all of this, soccer season was progressing. Although he didn't really play well at the beginning of the season, James was coming around pretty well towards the end. Then came another "Nana" encounter, which would change everything.

She Strikes Again

After the Facebook posts, she let up for about a month. Then, in March, she attempted to go and eat lunch with James. The school secretary had called to ask me, and I had said no. Then I received a letter in the mail from "Nana", telling me how she needed to see the boys and that I was damaging them. She implied that I had brainwashed them. I ignored it, but knew that further problems were imminent. I was worried everywhere we went. I thought she might show up at any event at any time. It took her about a month and a half to make the next move, but it was a big one. She called the elementary school, and they mailed her a copy of the upcoming events for the month.

There were not any out-of-the-building events, so she decided to make a personal visit to the school and obtain the following month's event schedule. She figured out when and where he would be during a field trip to a local park for some school music performance. "Brown Bag Concerts" are annual events during the spring before school lets out. I usually attend, and had never seen her at any of them in the past. The field trip for my preschool class ended up being on the same day, so I could not attend. I had a thought about her showing up, but felt like I was crazy for being so paranoid. I guess I should have known. She showed up, approached James, took his picture, and went on her way. The school didn't even know that she had been there, despite my clear warnings to be mindful. When I spoke to the teacher, she said that she had seen someone talking to him, but didn't question it. It was the first thing James told me when I saw him after school. When I discussed it with the school staff, they didn't have much to say about it. They didn't even know that she was there, and they kept saying how it was a public place. At that time, I didn't know that they had actually provided her with the date and time of the event- that was not something that they shared with me.

Immediately, James reverted back to some of the behaviors that I hadn't realized had been improving. Although he had actually been playing soccer as part of the team, not just running around without purpose, he regressed. He went back to hopping around outside the group of kids on the field, rather than playing the game. He got "color changes" (for behavior at school) the days following the interaction with her. He went back to galloping and flapping all of the time. This solidified my decision in choosing a qualified, experienced therapist, and we embarked on our journey to healing.

I filed for another protection order the day after the encounter at the park. No lawyer this time. I was out of funds. I went to the hearing on my own. She cried, she told of how she "helped" me get the boys. She told her sad story that her husband was so horrible to her, which I found rather irrelevant to her approaching my son. I told my story. She had come with an attorney. Her attorney tried to make it seem as if I was the one harming the children, and that this poor woman had done nothing wrong. I couldn't believe it when I was handed a "motion to dismiss", and on it was the admission that she sought James out deliberately outside the classroom. She even detailed her efforts to obtain the schedule of events. Until that point, I figured she had just found out from someone that worked at the school, or simply taken the chance that he'd be there since his school (not his class) was performing. She actually admitted to getting the calendar sent, and then going to the school after the April calendar wasn't sufficient. It was the same judge as before, and although he gave me positive feedback the first time, this time he told me that he thought that I was wrong for what I was doing, but he granted the protection order.

I guess it didn't matter what he thought of me, so long as we were safe. He did not have much patience for her pleas, however, to be able to approach me and the boys in public settings. She actually asked him (after first being requested to go through her attorney) if she was able to seek us out at the local grocery store. She wanted to know what she was supposed to do if we happened to be there at the same time. He told her to turn around and walk away. She was not happy with that answer, and her face gave a clear message of her feelings about that. I could just picture her waiting in the parking lot of the only grocery store in town just for a chance to get at us. I was pleased that he left little doubt about the expectation to leave us alone entirely.

I felt so much relief. I knew it was only for a year, but I felt better about going in public and sending my son to school- sort of. The school staff were pretty nonchalant about the whole matter, and dismissed my concerns. They did not feel as if it was their responsibility to keep her away from a public place. I provided them with the protection order, and gave instructions to call the police if she came near the school. The secretary called the principal down to meet with me, and the principal took no responsibility for the fact that the former grandmother had approached my son due to information that was freely given to her upon request. I cried when I got back to the car. How could they not even apologize for their role? I had no intention of removing him from the school, though, as it was his second school in as many years. I didn't have to worry about dealing with that school again, anyway, as it turned out. I must have been too high-

97

maintenance as a parent, because several months later, before school would resume in the fall, our request for transfer to attend that school was denied. It was a blessing in disguise, as we've been very happy with the school we ended up with.

I received a notice of appeal in the mail within a month of the court hearing. I sought low-income legal services this time, and was provided with representation. I was only responsible for court fees and a few other things. The attorney I ended up with told me that he was usually given the "weird" cases. He struck me as an odd person, and a bit overconfident, but I knew I needed guidance, as I had little knowledge of the legal system. He was pretty impersonal, used foul language, and wore short colorful socks with his suit and dress shoes. I had no idea how to get through an appeal without an attorney, but looking back, I might have done just as well without one. He suggested I try to go for a different kind of restraining order- one that would be permanent, but didn't have the same guidelines, such as proving incidents of stalking. He may have been right about that, but our attempt to acquire it probably wasn't planned out so well.

In the meantime, the protection from stalking appeal was still ongoing. In that hearing, I displayed more emotion publically than I ever had. I was angry. It was one of those experiences that I wish I didn't remember. It felt like a poorly performed episode of a law show on TV. I still can't figure out if it would be considered comedy or drama. First, within 5 minutes of beginning, my attorney was nearly held in contempt by the judge. He was arguing with the judge, and not really doing very well, in my opinion. I finally spoke up, in a voice that I didn't know I had. I was scared, because I had heard judges very harshly speak to people in the courtroom. I said "May I please just tell what happened?" The judge (I heard later that I was very lucky because he is a "by-the-book" guy, and this wasn't exactly protocol) said "Well, somebody needs to!" I started talking. I told what happened, what she had done, trying very hard to speak without having a bunch of objections due to my references to the boys' statements. It was difficult. Then my attorney finally took over when I paused, and asked me what exactly made me feel scared about the former grandmother. That's when things really blew up. The opposing attorney chuckled and mumbled "That's what I'd like to know". My attorney, in his dorky dramatic way acted extremely appalled, and the judge went ballistic. That's when my outburst began- I am pretty sure I should have just kept my mouth closed, and heard whatever the judge had begun to say. I don't even know what I said anyway. I was shaking. I was mad. I was scared. I was lost for words. I honestly can't recall much of what I said, but I know it started something like this: "What am I scared of? I'll tell you what I'm scared of! I am scared this is never going to end. I'm scared that there is nowhere we can go to get away from her. I am scared that my son can't even go to school and be safe. I'm scared that she will keep doing this and my kids will never get better. I'm scared that my kids will never be able to have a feeling of safety and security. I don't know what to do. I am scared that she is going to do this forever!" I said a bunch of other stuff, too, but I can't begin to guess what actually came out of my mouth.

When I was done, I don't know how things went for a bit, but her attorney didn't interrupt by laughing again. He objected to some of my testimony, but many of his objections were overruled. When I was telling about the kids' reactions to her presence, he would object, but the visual descriptions I gave were admitted. The crazy woman, the former grandmother, actually brought evidence of the incidents I described. This puzzled me. Why would she bring the proof that she did what I said she did? She brought the photographs she took of my sons. She admitted that she went backstage to seek out my boys, she admitted that she went to the school to try and eat lunch with him (although she

99

lied about the initial intent and said that she was really only going there to eat with a friend who worked at the school- the "rules" were different from what she thought, she said, and that's why they called me), and she admitted to seeking my son out while he was on his field trip. My statement about the incident, saying that she sought him "when he was vulnerable by being outside of the school building" was objected to. Apparently her attorney had a problem with my use of the word "vulnerable". I rephrased to use "accessible" even before the judge could say anything.

I don't understand why she thought it would be acceptable to do these things. I thought it was really strange to admit the behaviors so openly. She didn't think her 100 texts within 2-3 weeks were too much. She didn't see a problem with seeking out my kids outside my presence, and against my wishes. She thought that she should be able to go backstage at any performance to chase them down. I thought for sure I was going to lose, because she was so open about these behaviors. I was beginning to be convinced that I was crazy for thinking that she shouldn't be able to do these things. My attorney had irritated the judge, and it's really hard to tell the whole story when nothing that my kids said could be used as evidence, and I couldn't use what the therapist said without having her present. When there was a crying grandmother on the stand trying to say how close she was with the boys, I ended up looking like a horrid heartless child-stealer. I thankfully won, but I don't know how. She began the process of appealing that, too, but did not go through with it.

The next hearing was for the restraining order that was different from the protection from stalking order. I was not looking forward to having to go to court yet another time. I lost that one, but without an attorney I think I would have won because the judge seemed to be basing his ruling on the fact that the protection order was in place, and so the attorney had chosen that route. The judge told the attorney that he should have chosen that type of order in the first place, and he had to stick with his first choice. The judge had no way of knowing that I was the one who filed the original protection order, without an attorney. I didn't know any different, and had no idea that there was a more appropriate type of restraining order. I only sought representation after the protection order was appealed. Regardless, I felt good leaving that hearing. He spoke very kindly- directly to me. He made sure that I knew that the difficulty I had experienced was not deserved, and very clearly referred to the former grandmother in that way- as the "former grandmother". He even specifically commented on it as he stated it- making it clear that her role as grandmother was no longer recognized. I felt validated as the boys' mother for the first time ever, and left there feeling as though I won, even though the court ruling was not in my favor.

Once again, I thought everything was over. I didn't really relax, but felt like we didn't have to face anything for a year. She had her attorney draw up an agreement that would provide for permission for her to "run into us" at places like the grocery store, and that I was to send her photographs and updates. I declined, because I honestly think that she would wait for us to create the "chance meeting". I did not want to set up a situation like that. She finally agreed to stay away from us permanently, with the understanding that I could use prior incidents as evidence if I needed to obtain protection in the future. The agreement included a provision that I was to cancel the protection order before the expiration. I did, and hopefully I will never have to enter a courtroom again. All of that legal process took place over a year and half. During that time, I was beginning to understand how truly damaged my sons were. The stress of addressing their needs, as well as contending with court issues, was extremely difficult to handle.

We began therapy shortly before the field trip invasion (before all of the court proceedings described were completed). It was mostly evaluations at that point. There were many behavior surveys to fill out, and history to provide. I was grateful that the therapist would see Jackson, too. I knew he wasn't a happy little guy, but would find out later that he was likely more wounded than James. He had seemed to make so much progress, while James just hadn't changed a lot since being with me. Therapy was different than I thought it would be. Even the evaluations stressed me out. Our interactions were observed, and I was nervous about doing the wrong thing. The boys acted out, as expected. They climbed the furniture, tore stuff up, and were downright naughty. The evaluations confirmed my suspicions that James was suffering from an attachment disorder, but opened my eyes to the depth of the problem. I hadn't considered childhood depression or Post Traumatic Stress Disorder as concerns. Although it seems odd to say, the diagnosis was welcome. I felt such relief knowing that it wasn't just them, and it wasn't just me. There was an awareness of greater problems, but there was a new sense of hope. We didn't have to suffer like this forever. I won't pretend that I suddenly became the mother they needed me to be, or that they miraculously recovered and their behavior was spectacular. It didn't happen like that. We would still have stories to tell. In fact, I think that our story was still just beginning. Our existence would soon become connected.

Therapy

When therapy began, it was most helpful for me, rather than the boys. There were a few things we needed to change right away. The first thing was the limiting of contact with biological family members. It is really strange how things played out as we began therapy. I didn't realize that the boys' behaviors while visiting their birthmother were avoidance and anxiety based behaviors. They were just naughty, as far as I knew. They would insist on playing games, much to my displeasure, and against my suggestions. They had to be provided with separate treats, which was extremely costly. I had finally gotten smart enough to bring in disposable cups with lids so they could split a bottle of soda pop. I was going broke and they were indulging in too much junk food. James displayed the worst behavior during visits. He would throw food and game pieces, and climb on things and people, and squeeze his birthmother. He'd jump on her, and he'd do anything I asked him not to. Once, after deliberately making a huge mess with his cheese puffs, he went to wipe his hands on his birthmother. She asked him not to, telling him she had just washed the shirt. He dug his hands into the bag, acting famished-trying to pick up the crumbs. Then he proceeded to wipe his hands down the entire length of the front of her shirt, laughing all the time. The biggest problem was that she was laughing all the while, too. She said "stop", but didn't really mean it. She would then attempt to say that it upset her, and give the appearance of being upset, very briefly. Then James would fall apart, attempting to melt into the floor. This would only last a short time, and then she would somehow get him back into the hyper, cackling mode.

On the last visit we had, (not knowing it would be the last) it was evident to me that the visits really were harmful. The boys *were* getting better, although it was hard to tell. James had gone for a couple of weeks without soiling himself before the "Nana" visit at the park, but was having trouble again. During this visit, we were finally permitted to visit outside, which had not been possible before. There were carport like shelters, and a small playground. James was acting strangely, and I thought that maybe he was dwelling on the field trip invasion, or was avoiding using the bathroom again. He had gotten under a part of the playground equipment and sat alone. He often sought out semi-secluded areas when he really needed to go to the bathroom, just like a potty-training toddler does. I asked him if he needed to use the bathroom, a common question, and he said no, but didn't respond with screaming. He said he just didn't feel right, but he wasn't sick. I said that it was OK, and that if he wanted to hang out there, I thought he was making a good choice. Usually, when upset, he would lose control and often damage things by being overly silly, or hurting Jackson.

During that same visit, their birthmother had picked up Jackson (who looked at me for reassurance) and was walking him around letting him look into the nests that birds had built in the corners of the metal shade structures. He went to put his hand in, and I told him not to touch them. His birthmother laughed as he reached in again. They went to another nest, and he, laughing, reached again to a nest, delighting the birthmother. They wandered through each shelter, and at each corner, Jackson would reach into a nest. Then the birthmother would giggle and say "no, don't touch". They had gone to several nests, with the same interaction at each one. At about the 5th nest, it looked like the same thing again, but instead of just reaching up to the nest, he grabbed an egg and dropped it on the ground, breaking it. There was a very underdeveloped dead bird lying on the ground, and immediately, shock struck Jackson. The birthmother, still laughing, but with disappointment in her tone, asked him "Why did you do that?"

My poor son realized what he had done. He saw the remains of the egg and its contents, and fell apart. James couldn't help but reiterate the fact that Jackson had killed the bird, and it wasn't going to live any more. We left that visit differently than we ever had. It was a somber exit. Jackson was so upset that he couldn't even look up. They didn't race up the stairs (as I always instructed them not to, but happened every time anyway), they sat on the bench while I signed out (also a standing never-respected request), and solemnly walked out to the car. James was the first to speak, and although he often provoked Jackson, I don't think he purposefully caused him to become more upset on this occasion. He said "I can't believe Jackson killed the bird". Jackson couldn't bear it. His face fell further, and he screamed silently with his mouth open before the wails began. I probably got after James for the statement, although I am not sure that it was the right thing to do. He was stating the obvious, as usual, and he had to do something to disrupt the feelings he was having himself. He had been feeling poorly before the incident with the bird. The visits were harmful.

Our therapist knew so much before we even had a chance to get started. Why hadn't I figured that out before? The signs were there, not typically quite as evident as that day, but they were there. I was finally seeing things more clearly. I explained that Jackson hadn't ever intended to hurt the bird. I told them both that things just happened that way. Their birthmother was laughing, and Jackson didn't realize that what he was doing wasn't really funny. I think it was the first time (and one of the only times) that I specifically made a statement that placed responsibility on their birthmother for contributing to a problem. The boys responded in a way that I didn't expect- especially James. It was a mature expression on his face, and he actually voiced an understanding of that very issue. I just wish I had stopped things before they had gone that far- even if only for that day with the nests. I saw it happening. I should have stopped it. I may not have realized that a bird would die, or that my son would weigh himself down with guilt over that incident. He was only 4 years old. An adult was encouraging him to continue his behavior by laughing and giving him the opportunity to engage in the behavior. It was not his fault. I remember my voice shaking as I tried to explain that to the boys. I was so distraught.

Looking at my sons, I was overcome with emotion. I saw James shut down immediately following his very short, yet meaningful assertion that he realized that it shouldn't have happened that way. Then his favored mode of protection set in and the emptiness of an avoidant child was all that was left. He couldn't even look at me, and was not crying or showing much emotion at all. He went into his "fake happy" mode and started making noises and asking redundant questions. He couldn't cope with all that was going on, so he was trying to distance himself from it. For some reason, that visit had bothered him even before the egg had cracked- figuratively and literally. He had witnessed the whole thing with Jackson and his birthmother, and I, at the very least, stated his name with exasperation when he reminded us, (as if we could have forgotten) about the dead bird at the hands of his brother. Then there was Jackson, slumping as low as he could in his seat (only to be held in by the harness). He looked as if he carried enough shame and hurt to last him a lifetime. No little boy could have grieved with more pain. His whole body, all

38 pounds of it, displayed a greater sense of hopelessness than I've ever seen in anyone. My words of encouragement and attempt at reasoning did nothing to relieve his burden. He, I'm sure, felt as if he was the worst person in the world. I don't know if the boys saw my tears as I wiped them away when we started for home. I can't help but think that the visit that day, while a memory we'd all like to forget, was a turning point for us. We started from there. Therapy was beginning, and we were going to move forward. An understanding of the negative influence of their birthmother was developing. I think it began for all of us at the same time. It was time to move on.

All In

I knew it was going to be hard to tell their birthmother that we were no longer going to visit. It was. She handled it remarkably well, and still does. It's hard on her, and on me. I feel bad, because at the time of the adoption I implied that I would allow her access to the children so long as she wasn't engaging in dangerous behavior (like back into drugs). I didn't realize at the time that the visits were causing the boys harm. Without hesitation, the boys are my priority, and they need to be healthy and happy. The problem remains that I can't help but feel guilty about how the visits suddenly stopped, and she was no longer able to see the boys. If there could be a way to allow her to visit that didn't harm the boys, I'd be all for it. There is not, so we continue the same way. The guilt remains, but the reality of the situation persists, as well. I continue to try and help her pull through and be successful, but my efforts must not interfere with the boys' progress. It's very difficult to do, and, as evidenced in my confessions, I am not always completely successful.

We began therapy at the end of our first spring together, just before summer. Leaving work every Friday afternoon for a 2-hour drive was difficult. After the evaluations were done, and a treatment plan in place, I tried to work up enough nerve to ask our therapist the question that had been keeping me up at night. I hesitated while leaving during one of our first sessions. James had pushed Jackson into a thorny bush just outside the office, and Jackson was bleeding. I was trying to console him, and keep James from being run over in the parking lot. I had tried to ask a couple of times before that, but I couldn't get the words out. I finally did. I asked "Is it too late? Are they really going to be OK?" My heart was pounding as I awaited her answer. I had fully accepted the diagnosis, and come to terms with the fact that the boys had serious problems. I had also become very aware of their behaviors and the significance of them. Even though I almost wish I hadn't, I'd looked up a lot of information on RAD and PTSD in children. What I read was incredibly enlightening... and scary. As I awaited her response, I began to imagine how I would respond if I didn't get the answer I wanted. How could we go through life, without a sense of certainty? Would my hope be lost if I knew the possibility of failure? Our therapist gave me the answer I wanted. She said that they would be fine. Whether that was a compulsory response, I'll never know. All I know is that I *needed* that statement. I needed to know that everything we were working for was not in vain.

Fortunately, we were able to make it through the spring, as I was given a new sense of accomplishment. I had signed James up for baseball before therapy began, and the summer was hectic. He struggles with confidence still, but at that time, his self-concept was even worse, so sports where individual efforts are noted were difficult for him.

Then there was the issue with the deadly weapon (most people would probably call it a baseball bat) he held in his hands. The proximity to other children while holding the bat terrified me. I must have looked insane while constantly seeking him out to tell him to get the bat down and move away from other kids. I don't honestly know how we made it through the season without him busting someone's head open, or me having a panic attack. Other people didn't see the same thing I did. They saw a little boy with a baseball bat. I saw an "accident" waiting to happen. I replay the images in my head, even now, and am grateful that no one was hurt. I am sure that he looked like any other little boy to everyone else. They hadn't witnessed the calculated schemes to injure his little brother. They hadn't seen him throw balls so hard at people, with the only intent being to make contact with someone. They hadn't been around when he found objects for weaponry everyplace we went. They hadn't caught a glimpse of the faraway look and apparent pleasure while attempting to squeeze a frog to death. No one else heard him speak of killing, murdering, stabbing, shooting, slicing up, smashing heads in, or taking brains out of people and animals, with such frequency and pleasure that it was sickening to me. They didn't witness him have no sense of control with anything, and the apparent pleasure he had when others experienced pain. He was unable to use any object for its *intended* purpose, but nobody else really understood that. There he was, a sweet-looking little boy swinging a baseball bat, and here I was, the crazy mother who needed to be committed.

James once cut in line and spit on another child during practice, laughing all the while, and repeatedly went after the ball when it wasn't his turn. Twice during this same practice, (they were practicing near the batting cages because the field was occupied) he ran into the road into oncoming traffic. I was both calmed and terrified when I realized that a coach and another parent were also in a panic over his especially close call. After my heart started beating again, I felt an odd sense of satisfaction. It was nice that others were in agreement with me, for once, as I feared for my son. I felt as if everyone always viewed me as obsessively overprotective and insanely paranoid. Here was the one time for me to be joined in my concern for my son. I went to the coach to apologize afterward- mostly for when James was going after the balls intended for other children, and the spitting he had done on the children in the vicinity, but I got the "crazy mom" look. My kid was "fine", according to them- just as everyone always said. "All kids do that". That phrase, which came to be very commonly spoken to me, I would soon dread to hear.

Although I was keeping an eye on James, praying that he wouldn't hit anyone with that bat, baseball practice gave Jackson and me some time together to play without James. James made play absolutely impossible. Jackson, though, was going through a (very long) stage of complete defiance and opposition. Whatever I said, he did the opposite. It was quite stressful, and no one can wholly understand how impossible things could be as a result of this type of behavior without having experienced it. Once, during one of the practice times, Jackson and I were at the playground. He wanted to go on the swings, and I was pushing him. He said he wanted to go higher, and of course, being the servant I was, I obliged. Instinctively, I said "Hold on tight!" as I gave him a big push towards the sky. My son, determined in his opposition, didn't "hold on"... he let go. He fell backwards, landing right on his head. He immediately began screaming, and I was almost scared to move him for fear that he had broken his neck. I was relieved to find that he wasn't seriously wounded. Fortunately he had landed where the ground cover was sufficient, so his injuries were minor- no blood or big bump. I wish I could blame that incident on Jackson's lack of knowledge; conceptual confusion- something that he might develop an understanding for in the future, but he's a smart kid. He was just so adamant to go against what I said that he couldn't think rationally. How a child can be so completely obsessed with the idea of being oppositional that he would let go of a swing in response to being told to "hold on" is beyond me. Then again, that's just the way life went for us at that time.

111

James struggled with baseball, wanting to do well, yet not putting enough effort into trying. If he tried, then he had to live with the possibility of failing. This was the battle, and he could not overcome the fear of failure. He would rather look like a fool than give an honest attempt at success. He actually played better at the beginning of the season, as opposed to the end. He hit the first couple of times at bat, but then didn't really ever hit again. After striking out, he just gave up. His throwing and catching left a lot to be desired, as well. Taking into consideration that his body was in a constant state of rigidity, and his age and experience, he wasn't a terrible player- he just didn't have the confidence to try to be better. Then came the foul ball. He made contact with the ball in one of the final games, quite by accident. It was a solid hit, but foul. His head appeared to grow to the size of a hot air balloon. He gave the impression of extreme confidence and pride in his own spectacular athletic ability.

I had such a hard time dealing with this specific issue. Maybe it was because I was already worn down. This conflict was not new. He went back and forth between praising himself and practically demanding recognition of his somewhat insignificant accomplishments. He would not discuss anything that he actually had talent for, however, and would engage in self-loathing behaviors alternately with making statements that appeared to be signs of overconfidence.

Once, before therapy began, there was one of those instances that exemplified his awkward method of self-praise and apparent need for recognition to perfection. He was coloring a picture- a detailed ocean scene. In a matter of 15 minutes, that child spent more time seeking approval and praise for his work than he actually spent coloring. In this short period of time I'm referring to, I had attempted to use the bathroom and switch the laundry. He sought me out. He knocked on the bathroom door after he found it locked, asking me if I liked the color he chose for something. I, still behind the closed door, told him that I couldn't wait to see it. Not waiting for me to see the color, he walked away with the picture, saying "I am good at coloring. I think I am the best colorer in the world. Aren't I good at coloring?" Then he sat for maybe 10 seconds, scribbled in a small sea animal, and said "Do you like this? I made it look really good. I think it's the best one ever! Isn't it good?" I don't actually think he was listening to my responses, but I thought he just needed a lot of reassurance. It was very annoying, however, and difficult to come up with a variety of ways to acknowledge his work. He would go back, color a little more, and seek me out again. Once, I was in the same room with him, and he left looking for me, not even realizing I was right there, and had actually been speaking to him. It was so odd that he was so completely in his own little world, while appearing to seek out others for a response. This behavior has persisted somewhat, but not to the extent that it once was.

Anyway, back to the foul ball... he had no problem informing everyone in the dugout that he was the best hitter on the team. "Did you see my foul ball?" "I'm probably the best hitter." "It almost went over the fence." "If it wasn't a foul ball, it would have been a home run!" Amazingly, not one of those kids set him in his place. They ignored him, mostly, but he didn't even seem to notice. It didn't help that the coach provided everyone who got a hit that game with a hot dog. He ran with the boys who had hit in the game to get one, and the coach obliged even though it really wasn't a "hit". I know that I should have been able to be happier for him, but it was hard. It wasn't just the fact that the "hit" was only a foul ball- it was also because the prize for a hit was a hot dog. That child had fits for hours over the mere thought of being served a hot dog. He had refused hot dogs every time offered him in the past, with no less than an hour long fit, even when hot dogs were just an *option*. The one college baseball game I had taken him to (which he left in a crying state because he didn't catch a foul ball) had hot dogs for $1 the night we were there, but I had to pay $4.50 for a burger he didn't eat half of.

So here we were. I was trying desperately to display positivity regarding that *impressive* foul ball, all the while boiling inside. He had darted through the ball field parking lot, again disregarding the approaching vehicles to obtain this prized reward for the foul ball- a dreaded hot dog he'd spent countless hours avoiding the sight of. I heard about that foul ball for the whole drive home, through what must have been half of the hot dog at a time in his mouth. Then he went on. And on. His questions were rhetorical, yet he answered himself. "Do you think I'm the best baseball player you've ever seen? I am really good at baseball. Would that have been a home run? That would have been a home run. I'm the best hitter on the team." I felt guilty wanting this apparent feeling of pride and success to just stop. Here he was grinning ear to ear, and I couldn't even be happy for him. Even without saying anything, I know my displeasure had to have come through. I didn't understand him then. I didn't realize that he felt so poorly about himself that he was trying to convince himself that he wasn't worthless.

Therapy helped me understand that concept way before any progress was made as far as his own feeling of self-worth. Although I desperately wish that therapy had helped him with that first, I don't think he could even begin to heal until I began to really know him. I knew "him", as others did, but it took a long time to see the real child beneath the mask. I considered myself to be knowledgeable when it came to understanding children. I was well educated, experienced, and knew a lot about children and behavior. I knew children. It should have been easy to make the connection with my own son, or so I thought. I found it very easy to become close to children, and never thought that there could be something preventing any child from developing a relationship. I was usually pretty good at keeping a calm atmosphere and working with even very difficult children.

I am embarrassed to say that as we were beginning therapy- not quite a year into our lives together, and 6 months post-adoption, I didn't really know my sons. I was becoming closer to Jackson, but he was seeming to have more difficult behavior at times. James was still distant. Fake. I couldn't tell if he'd had a bad day at school when he came home. I couldn't tell when he lied to me. I was completely ignorant to the fact that his behavior was screaming at me what his words couldn't express. He spent his time being scared, nervous, and self-conscious, and instead of understanding his behaviors, I viewed them as selfish, uncontrolled, and mean. I tried to be understanding. I just didn't know what I was supposed to be understanding. He was so hidden inside himself that I couldn't find the real child. He was a master at avoidance, and I played right into his hands. That's how I came to realize that while therapy was for both of the boys, it wasn't going to do anything unless the changes came through me. They needed someone- me- to understand them and help them through. I only wish I had been able to do that for them from the start.

Moving Forward

When therapy began, their behavior changed little, although I was feeling considerably better. I could let go of the doubt I had about the boys and their behavior, as well as my perception of them. They really did have problems that a professional could see. Our therapist deserves all of the credit, actually. She is simply an amazing person. I don't know how we possibly could have left that horrible life we were living and move forward without her. She gave me hope, without pretending that it would be easy. That's all I needed. I had been told time and time again by people close to me that the boys were fine. My poor mother was my sounding board. My sister was supportive at times, but I don't think she ever fully grasped the severity of the boys' problems. She gave me many of the "all kids do that" responses, or gave the impression that my sons' problems were not that big of a deal, as her kids struggled with things, too. Although I sensed that she felt that I was foolish for taking the boys to a specialist 2 hours away every week, she didn't say anything that harsh. I know she loves my boys, but she hasn't experienced the fits that go on for hours, or the behavior as a result of trauma triggers. She doesn't quite realize the significance in the fears that James has, or how his odd behaviors are actually related to his emotional disorder.

Once, shortly after starting therapy, we were at her house, visiting. The boys were on the trampoline, and it was only a month or two after James had been approached during that field trip. He was in his "galloping fairy" mode constantly. I'll admit- he was rather funny looking. We were talking about the boys, and I was probably mentioning how amazing the therapist was (probably how she seemed to know my children even before we met!). My sister, not meaning to be hurtful, jokingly said "therapy won't fix that!" I was only slightly offended by the statement, because, in all honesty, therapy would. His whole body was taken over by the trauma and fear in his life. He was completely rigid and avoidant, which made him look really odd. Therapy was certainly helping me to understand that, even if others were not able to.

Regardless, I looked like a fool most of the time, and although I wouldn't have thought that two little boys could be so calculating, they seemed to have an instinctive ability to create situations that others could view me unfavorably. I would listen to screaming fits for hours, only to have them turned off and pleasant behavior displayed at the sight of someone else. Since balls were banned in the house (from the start, but strictly enforced following shattered glass on more than one occasion), they would get a ball and appear to play very nicely with it- gently. I would give a reminder about "no balls in the house", and pitifully, they would whine and say "I guess we can't do anything." Then they would seek out something else that would be unacceptable. There is a game that *my* grandpa had made many years before- one with lots of marbles to lose. It was always a "no", unless I got it out for us to play (which didn't really happen, since they couldn't play anything). This would be another option for them to try and get out while we had company. Then something really noisy would be next- a plastic recorder, one of those noisy trucks with buttons, something with great volume.   When I would discourage that,

117

stuffed animals might come into play- and be thrown in my face. Or somehow they would find something that should have been out of their reach- a laser pointer, permanent markers, scissors, someone's phone, a screwdriver- anything that would be off limits and only left available by accident (or they somehow managed to retrieve it from the place I thought was safe). I could name 50 things that would be fine to do- games, puzzles, books, coloring, Legos, small cars with tracks, foam blocks, anything- but they would find the few things would be inappropriate to do at that time. I would be the one saying "no", and being told all the while "they're just kids", "all kids do that", and "you have to let them do something". My brother, having two sons himself, didn't quite get it either. His wife was worse, making it clear that she didn't believe in the whole "therapy thing". My brother's implications hurt more, though. I cared deeply about what he thought.

One night he called me on the phone, just as I had put the boys to bed. They didn't often allow me to talk on the phone without interruptions, and that night was no exception. Jackson was in his overly demanding phase and had been shouting that he wanted another hug. I got after him, and said that I loved him, but he could not get another hug. The child had kicked me no less than 5 minutes prior as I had succumbed to his requests for an additional hug- before my brother had called. I was not about to be kicked again. My brother, caring as he is, felt that my refusal to hug that "poor child" was just terrible. He lectured me on how I should "never withhold love" like that. Seriously. I had been abused by that child every second we spent together that day. He had been hugged more than once, and had kicked me as I tried to give him his second hug. Jackson didn't need another hug. He didn't even want another hug. He just wanted the opportunity to control me and likely, exert his physical presence and kick or hit me. I stuck to my guns, and didn't give in to more hugs that night, but I had to overcome the overwhelming sense of guilt I was feeling. The hardest part was thinking over the words that my brother had spoken. I had to reassure myself that I did know what was best for my kids. My brother had no idea about the way our lives were at that point. His kids asking for another hug had a very different meaning than when my kids asked for hugs. His were seeking affection, comfort, love. Mine sought opportunity for aggression and control. The sets of brothers, now considered cousins, had very different intentions when requesting hugs- or anything else, for that matter.

Understanding

I began to feel really disappointed in myself, and confused. I went back and forth about blaming myself and feelings of inadequacy as a parent, and fully believing that my children were exceptionally difficult. It was likely a dangerous combination of both. The kids were difficult- more so than other children. I also wasn't meeting the needs that they had. It wasn't due to a lack of effort. I tried to be the best parent I could, and took on more than my fair share of hurt in return. Everything I did would result in less than positive reactions. I spent my time trying to deal with the disappointment from failing at my constant attempts to make them happy. When I wasn't protecting them from themselves (and each other), I was doing the things that I thought we should do to enjoy ourselves as a family. I would play games with them, but it always ended in disaster. I don't think we actually finished a game until nearly two years after we'd been together.

They couldn't play. I thought that play was practically an innate ability. Jackson was a little better with it, but James couldn't play at all. Everything turned violent. There was no turn taking. There had to be a winner, and it had to be him. He would cheat to beat his little brother at everything. I found it kind of funny the first time he had to give up because Jackson had learned to compensate so much that he was actually faster and better at things than James. James wouldn't try anything if he wasn't the best. His idea of playing ball was to throw or kick the ball as hard as he could to injure Jackson. Sticks became the first "off limits" thing outside. I got such dirty looks from people (mostly family), when they heard me say "no sticks" upon going outside. The looks got worse when they actually picked up the sticks, to defy me, giving a display of innocence to everyone else. I got the "all little boys play with sticks" conversation. They didn't understand that my little boys weren't just any little boys. Mine had the motivation to injure. Especially James. He did not seem to realize (or care) that he could injure people. He tackled, he poked, threw things at, and pushed others constantly. I was a wreck. I began to think that maybe this was just the way he was.

I saw, though, that he had so many other things going for him. He was smart, although he acted as if he wasn't. I couldn't figure out how someone so bright would not be able to understand that his actions were injuring people. I didn't realize that even if he did know he was hurting others (which is debatable), he didn't have the capacity to care. He was a hurt little boy, and did not have any way to cope with it. He was injurious to others as a result. He would grab people so hard that it would hurt. He would run and jump on someone as a greeting. It was so difficult to help him through that kind of behavior, especially since other people's reactions were involved. He would get the idea that it was sort of OK from others, even if they were choking out the words "let go, James", with a forced smile. My displeasure was probably the most appealing. It was a great game.

They also could not stay within any type of boundary. If we were in line at a store, and James was out of the cart, he was in other people's stuff, or in the cashier booth. He had no sense of acceptable space. The concept of staying in a yard was just not something he could grasp. I thought that the edge of the grass was a perfectly good boundary line. It wasn't. "Between the two

121

trees" wasn't any better. No matter how I put it, they could not stay in the yard. They would be around the back of the house, in the street, or in the neighbor's yard in the blink of an eye. I'd have them come in every time, but time and time again, the boundary was tested. My patience was tested, as well, because having to go inside was met with fits lasting at least an hour. In stores, they had to be placed in a cart- no matter how quick the trip. Every time I thought we might manage without one, I regretted the choice.

Once, when it was unbelievably cold, I had to go to the pet store for just one thing. I opted against the cart, especially since the carts there were small, and the last time I'd been at the pet store, and needed to use the bathroom, they had tipped the cart over on themselves before I had opened the bathroom door. It was a single restroom, and there was no one to keep them. I had said to sit still, and actually had James out of the cart, thinking that it might be safer, as he was always jerking the cart around while inside. I put the cart right next to the hall to enter the restroom, beside the fish that they always ask to look at. I turned around to open the door, and heard a great crash. I looked around the corner to find the cart tipped over, on top of James with Jackson falling out of the seat. How no one was hurt, I'll never know. I, needless to say, decided that I'd rather wait to use the bathroom as opposed to leaving them unattended for even a second.

This time, the pet store scene was just as memorable. As I waited in line- and the person in front of me was taking forever with some kind of confusion, the boys ignored my requests, then demands, to come near me. They were having a grand time going near the automatic door, causing it to open and allow a big draft of extremely frigid air inside. This, inside the pet store that has a sign noting their vigilance for efficiency by utilizing natural light during peak daylight hours. My kids were ignoring me entirely, while I held a 40 lb. bag of litter in my hands. What a fool I was. The cashier was looking at me funny, and the coupon I had was nowhere to be found, but I didn't even want to mess with it. I left as quickly as I could. It was a long time before I attempted without a cart again, and I have yet to attempt to shop without a cart and not regret the choice. Some things are just hard.

I couldn't leave them alone for a split second. I have no idea how they could find trouble so easily. They could, though. Simple things like silverware became weapons, or tools for damage. They could move in stealth mode to go to an off limits area in the blink of an eye. They would destroy things before I could get the words out to tell them to stop! Once, when I forgot something inside at my work, I went across the yard- about 40 feet, in the door about 10 feet to the refrigerator, and back out to the car. When I got back in the car, I smelled root beer. I looked behind me, and they were soaking wet, as was the entire backseat of the car, the ceiling of the car, and the windows. They had to-go cups with lids from a restaurant, and had discovered, in the matter of 30 seconds, that they could shake the cup with the ice being slammed against the lid, and the watery root beer would be forced out in droplets all over. It was a root beer sprayer. I wish I could have been impressed with their ingenuity, but I still haven't come to that point.

As if the mess weren't enough, when the game was ended, on account of the fact that I returned to the car, Jackson realized he was wet and sticky. He could not deal with being wet and sticky, so the ride home was quite loud and tense. Upon returning home, I got so wrapped up with the screaming sticky mess, I forgot to bring in the item I'd needed from the refrigerator until hours later. Needless to say, it had spoiled. That's the way life went at that time.

We were just miserable. It was so bad. I was upset all of the time, as were the boys. I don't know which was harder: dealing with the boys' difficult behavior, or feeling watched and criticized constantly over our interactions. The boys had a way of making everything difficult, and I just couldn't figure out how to avoid playing into their hands. They were good at that. We had little fun, and when I thought we were having fun, they would ruin it within minutes. Everything I tried was sabotaged, or begun with such difficulty that by the time the boys finally came around, we were all so upset that it wasn't fun at all. Little things like playing in the leaves, washing the car, playing in the sprinkler, going to the garden, playing in the snow- any new experience would begin with such a fit that I wanted to cry myself. At that time, I was idiotic enough to say things like "I have a surprise for you!" I soon learned that no anticipation was much better. When they found out the surprise, no matter what it was, they would both have a complete meltdown. I would be so excited to have gotten things ready for them- little rakes for leaves, their own sponges and buckets to "help" wash the car, a sprinkler to run through- and I'd be ready with my camera. Then I'd get crushed. I realize that there wasn't much I could have done differently at the time, but the hurt remains. I wanted to make them happy. I would get so excited, which made the disappointment at their distress so much harder to take. It was a really difficult time.

I had so much hope for them, and was so eager to give them the life they deserved, that their dissatisfaction with everything was nearly impossible to cope with. I didn't give up, but without our weekly therapy sessions, I don't know how much longer I could have gone. I just kept at it, getting knocked down again and again. I would try to make things equal and fair, but whatever I had arranged was wrong. Each event that should have been happy was so much the opposite that I began to question why I even tried to do anything for them. I was so excited for their first holidays with me, and the outcome was never as I had imagined. Each event turned into disaster. One or the other would be making us all miserable. James was best at ruining things like that. My mom had put a few coins in Easter eggs for a hunt with the cousins. James "only" got one quarter. He had a tantrum right there in the yard. I was displeased with his reaction and apparent ungratefulness, but I became furious when the cousins, only trying to help, gave him their coins. He immediately turned on a grin, and was just as pleased as punch. He acted as if he deserved those coins. It didn't matter to him a bit that other people might have wanted them. He didn't care. The complete mood change ability still persists, but isn't quite as extreme or frequent.

James was such a puzzle. He could appear to be fine, and change at the drop of a hat. I have many things I love about him, and could name them even then. However, James was likely the most annoying child I had ever met. He was simply an expert at annoying behaviors. He could manage to say "Hi" 4 times within 30 seconds. He would just say it again, and again. Mostly to me, using my name. It came to drive me nuts! Then there was the question game. He still plays it, but I'm not as dumb as I used to be. I used to fall for it much more often. He'd ask the same question again and again, but that didn't bother me near as much as asking the questions he already knew the answers to. Even though this behavior has kept up, it doesn't get to me the way it used to. I can call him out on it. "Where are we going?" as we're driving into the parking lot anyplace. "Are we eating supper?"- as I'm setting it on the table. My favorite was "Is that for me?" while I poured milk into his glass for supper- the same way I did every night. It was relentless. I got really annoyed when I would pour one glass first, and the other child would start having a fit because he wasn't getting milk. The same kind of response would come from me every night- that I didn't have two pitchers to pour from at the same time. If you didn't know any better, you'd think that I really would leave one of them out.

It was like that with a lot of things. Any time one was served first- it was worse with James, though- there would be a question of whether or not the other child would get any. With Jackson it was almost the opposite, many times. Rather than be concerned about being left out, he was not going to consume anything that James wasn't also provided with. It became really hard to do much of anything if Jackson was being given something first. He wouldn't even take a toy if James wasn't getting one, too. James would take both his and the one intended for Jackson without giving it a second thought. That angered me so much. I gave Jackson a marshmallow once right after a bath- I think because he hadn't soaked me with water, or he at least stopped when I asked him to. Small victories. Anyway, when I gave him the marshmallow, he asked if James was going to get one, too. I said something like "only if he does what he needs to". Jackson would not eat that marshmallow, and waited until he was sure that James was going to get one, too. James would not share a thing with Jackson, even when directly told to. James gave the impression that he was king, and Jackson was nothing. It was so sad.

James would hurt Jackson every chance he got. He would "play" so rough that Jackson would get hurt. He would break his toys, and take something Jackson wanted just so he couldn't have it. He was truly the meanest brother I'd ever seen. He would tell him that he was going to pick one thing, then, after Jackson had picked the same thing, James would get something different and tell how much better what he chose was. Jackson was always being hurt- physically and emotionally. No wonder the poor kid gave me the "I hate you" face all of the time. He felt like the whole world was against him.

Jackson still has trouble with feeling like he isn't worthy of anything, but it's coming along. I do remember the first time that I felt like he acknowledged my care for him. He had gotten a bump on the head, and I was being very gentle washing his hair. He commented on it, and I didn't think too much of it. When Valentine's day came, I was asking the boys what "love" was- a question I use in my classroom when it's that time of year, too. Most kids say "kisses", "hugs", "my mom", "my mom takes care of me", things like that. James couldn't say a thing. He cried because I was trying to get him to say something- anything. Jackson was good at it. He could say things like "she takes care of me", or "getting me new games", "letting me play my games", etc. The one that stuck out to me, though- was when he said that he knew I loved him because I was "very careful when I washed his head so it wouldn't hurt". I nearly cried as we drove home that day. I'm pretty sure that there were some "I hate you" face moments upon our arrival at home, but that was the norm at that time. My son verbalizing (without pronouncing his "r" sound, and saying "ooo" for "you") that he knew I loved him because of my care- that was certainly not something that happened normally during that time. It was extraordinary.

Jackson demonstrated an understanding about others' needs. He displayed empathy, and recognized emotions. In those ways, he was so much further along than James was. James just couldn't do those kind of things. He couldn't take another perspective in any way, shape, or form. He was completely self-absorbed. It was disastrous!

The boys were amazing at being able to manipulate any situation or just make things difficult. James, a very bright child, would play the "I'm dumb and incompetent" game constantly. He couldn't figure out how to get his pants on, then he couldn't figure out how to get his pants off. I remember one specific incident following a baseball game where James was getting ready for a bath. He started to take off his baseball pants with the cleats still on. Needless to say, it wasn't going to work. I was determined to get him to figure the problem out (although he knew what he was doing from the start). I began to doubt his intelligence from time to time during these kind of episodes, but he just knew how to play the game really well. He honestly would have stayed there screaming all night "I can't get my pants off, I don't know how!" if I would have let him. If other people weren't around to hear him screaming, I probably would have. I had to give in. Immediately the screaming ended. He was happy and content. There was no "recovery time"- he was just all of a sudden fine. I'd come to call this phenomenon "The James Show". It would happen again and again- first an all-out fit over something, then the sudden end with a "that was easy" kind of statement. He was all smiles then.

It could be over anything. I might ask him to turn the light off, and the response would be "where is it?"- even though he was perfectly confident in knowing where the light switch was. He asked "Which clothes are mine?" for at least a year after I got him when he saw the clothes lying out for them. I would put them in the same place every day, and aside from Jackson's being considerably smaller, his stack would have a set of underwear on it because he wore a pull-up at night. James seemed oblivious to this, and even when I made him figure it out, he would inevitably go to the wrong set first. It was aggravating at first, but I finally found the humor in the situation. It took a really long time to find humor, and I still have trouble applying it when necessary.

Surviving

Shortly after beginning therapy, I found a house. We went through the process of buying our new home, which was extremely challenging in and of itself. I didn't tell the boys until I was absolutely sure things were final. I didn't want to have them be disappointed if something fell through. My financial situation was tight, and I qualified for a loan, but it was a short-sale. I had to make the repairs required for the home myself. I had to paint the eaves, repaint a bathroom, get some plumbing and electrical work done, and clean out the refrigerator which had been taken over by mold. It was a big job, and I did everything I could without a contractor. Plumbing, inspections, and termites were the only things I had to pay for services for. My brother, thankfully, is a licensed electrician, and helped me out with that. At that time, the court hearings were quite frequent, as well. I honestly do not know how we survived that spring and summer. The "stress factors" in my life were completely off the charts. I was so preoccupied with the possibilities and uncertainty that I was a wreck. It sure didn't help my patience any.

As if the stress of everything going on wasn't enough, I was having to deal with the guilt from having a short fuse. I had a very difficult group of school-age children all day at work, only to come home to my extremely difficult sons. We couldn't get out of the house in the morning without a fit. We couldn't get to work without a fit. We couldn't get in the car from daycare without a fit. We couldn't drive home without a fit. Supper was just one giant fit, as was the rest of the evening.

The food issues during this time cannot be described by any words that I have in my vocabulary. Mealtimes were torture. It didn't matter what food was served, or if nobody was going to be required to eat anything. I did not want the boys to use food as a source of control, but they could make anything an issue of control. My contention was that a taste of anything would not kill anyone. Any person near our home on any given evening during that time might argue that it sure sounded like someone being killed. Mashed potatoes were out of the question. I would put a dot of potatoes about the size of a pea on the plate for James. He would scream, run, kick, and howl. I would remove him from the table, and he'd scream louder. If he finally ended up at the table again, the peace would last less than 2 seconds, and he'd look at the plate and run again. It was the same thing, day after day. He would try nothing new, and anything he happened to seem to enjoy would be a sure miss the next time it was served. He was NOT eating that. I didn't necessarily mind letting him be hungry if he chose not to eat, but with his control over bowel movements being so excessive, eating fruit was something I insisted upon. He would wait so long to use the bathroom that he would practically stop eating anyway. I joked with my mom that I thought that adopting a 6 year old meant that we would be past potty training and poopy pants, but I didn't miss the baby time after all! It was a constant battle. When I thought we were doing well, the problem would resume again, and stick around for a long time. The food issues were terrible for even longer, though. I thought we'd never get over that.

At this time, things were completely exasperating on a daily basis. I couldn't please the kids, and it came to the point that they couldn't please me either. I was not in a good state of mind. I was trying so hard to make things go well, and nothing worked. Jackson was a mess. We were getting better about being in the car, but trouble was seldom absent. It was almost like he had a switch that was activated by my voice. Anything I said was wrong. He would ask things that he knew the answer to, just because he wanted to have a fit. My response meant little. It might be about whether it was time to eat, if he could play with something, if he could have candy, anything. I could say yes, and he'd have a fit. I could say no, and he'd have a fit. I would try to sugar coat things to avoid it, but nothing worked. I didn't even want to answer most of the time. I didn't know what to do, but the fit was almost a guarantee. It was a pain. I learned not to prepare the children with notice for anything, which would, at the very least, delay the inevitable tantrums.

Both boys had the ability to elevate my stress level without having fits, too. James could be extremely annoying, and although I love him with all my heart, I really wanted him to just stop talking sometimes. He made so much chatter with absolutely no purpose that I don't know how he didn't lose his voice. The same, repetitive questions were getting on my nerves. Jackson was also skilled at trying my patience. He would do something that I had just asked James to stop doing. It was usually a very minor issue- like a request to stay on the sidewalk, or not touch something. These "little" issues caused me to be very bitter. I was feeling criticized by everyone around, and realize that I'm sure I looked like a fool. I really was overreacting to these minor behavior challenges. I feel very poorly about myself when I think about those times. I was overreacting to the seemingly insignificant behavior problems that I just described. The problem wasn't just the annoying behaviors. The problem wasn't really the behaviors, at all. Some things, I realize now, might have been related to other problems, but not everything. James, from time to time, might have been chattering out of anxiety, but I have a hard time believing that he couldn't have come up with a different nonsense question. He asked me "How old are you?" at least 1,000 times. I'm not exaggerating. Jackson, too, wasn't just stepping off the sidewalk by "accident". The purpose wasn't to break a rule by stepping off of the sidewalk. The intent was to get at me. It wasn't like he just did that one thing. His whole purpose in life seemed to be to defy me, and he was determined to do so every minute of every day.

I can understand how others might have been seeing me. I know I looked mean. I felt mean. Even though I understood that the behaviors I addressed were not really bad, the purpose behind them was different for my children compared to others. I find it difficult to explain, but it's a hard way to live. I found myself addressing the little behaviors with less and less patience as time went on. It wasn't necessarily that the boys were all that *bad*. It was just that they were relentless, and they seemed to have keen instincts to be able to push every button I had. I really must have looked like a fool. I sure felt like one.

I tried to avoid power struggles, but every method I'd used in my classroom failed miserably. I would say "Which shoe do you want to put on first?" This no-lose request was met with either adamant refusal, or a special effort to find the one pair of shoes I didn't want worn. The brown dress shoes or sandals, for example, did not need to be worn with jeans. If I had requested them to be worn, the request would have been met with opposition, too. I had to become smarter. I had to hide the shoes I didn't want worn. I had to make sure that there was really no way to avoid compliance. I felt like everything I was doing was wrong. I kept thinking of all the things I'd learned about children-giving choices, providing options, teaching independence. I finally realized that these ideas, while appropriate for most young children, were not suitable for mine. I had to do everything differently for my children. It seemed like I was moving backwards. Everything I needed to do was opposite what I had learned. That phrase "give an inch, they'll take a mile" must have been created for children like mine.

Fun

Because our therapist was so far away, we would stay the night in a hotel sometimes. We would be forced to when winter came, but occasionally stayed overnight regardless of the season. I would look for things to do when we were there. Once, early on, I saw that the air museum was having a special event, and there would be many airplanes that people could actually go inside of and view. I was so happy to be able to bring my boys to something like that. I thought that they would be overjoyed. I had planned it out very carefully. I had originally planned to do the zoo, but when I found out about the special day at the air museum, I figured we had better take the opportunity. The planes were not available to get on very often- it wasn't even an annual event. I dressed them in the same color- to spot them easily if they ran off. I looked up the hours, admission, and kids activities available. I was really excited.

We were at the hotel, and I had told the boys that we were doing something special before we went home. They appeared excited at first, and started guessing- but nothing really very likely. I finally told them the "surprise", but the real "surprise" was their reaction. I said "We're going to go see real airplanes! We can go inside them- not flying, but you can even go sit where the pilot sits. Isn't that cool?" I was like a little kid telling what

Santa had brought (not one of my little kids, of course, but a normal little kid). Right before my eyes, they both immediately went into fits! Not excited, happy to go somewhere cool fits. These were falling on the floor screaming, moaning, kicking fits. I stood there in shock for a moment or two. I was confused. What had I said? What had I done wrong? Didn't all little boys like airplanes?

I was so tempted not to go to the air museum any more. I finally got them to stop bawling, but they were in *foul* moods. They really didn't want to go. James was pouting and mad. Jackson was angry and screaming off and on.

Once I finally got them in the car, I decided to go ahead and go, because I had gotten *myself* so excited about seeing the planes. James pouted the whole way there, giving dirty looks out the window. Jackson was like a little tiger. You wouldn't want to get close to him. He demanded a drink. I got one out of the cooler, and then he screamed because the ice water dripped off and made him cold. He didn't take a sip, and ended up leaving the juice box to be ruined in the car. I was having second thoughts as we parked. I asked them if they'd ever even seen an airplane, and of course, they hadn't. James, trying not to look too interested, began taking long looks at the aircraft around. Jackson insisted on finishing his fruit snacks before exiting the car. Anything to be difficult. We finally got in, and they were pulling on my arms in opposite directions as we waited in line for tickets. I was thinking to myself how crazy I was to be doing this. Everyone else around seemed to either be older people alone, or families with a mom and a dad. Then there was me, with my sons pulling my arms out of their sockets. I picked up Jackson, but he was not having much of that. The threat of being carried was enough to get him to straighten up a little. James finally became interested in what was around, and got himself together, too. After we finally got in, and started checking out the exhibits and the aircraft, the experience was quite pleasant. Getting to that point, however, was certainly a challenge.

I never really understood the fits that would occur when I let them know about "fun" plans. Jackson actually threw himself down on the floor of the hotel room when he heard me say "Let's go to the candy store!" I was taking them to a museum, and realized that it was very close to a candy store I liked to go to. Even knowing that the concept of "fun" was foreign to them, I struggled with the rejection, time and time again. Jackson was worse about it, but both boys had a hard time enjoying anything, and would display such extreme negativity in anticipation of "fun", that it seemed impossible to overcome. I would get so upset with myself for setting myself up to be hurt. I wanted to have fun with my children, but they could not have fun. I wanted to be excited to take them to new places. I wanted to create memories. Fun memories. It just wasn't possible. I didn't give up trying, but I wouldn't be telling the truth if I didn't consider it. My attempts to have "fun" with the boys left us all upset. I would feel so incredibly hurt after failing, yet again, to please them.

One of the moms from the support group thought that the boys' reaction might be because they felt like the good thing that was being promised would not actually happen, so the children must oppose the idea so as to avoid disappointment when the promise is broken. I guess it's a logical explanation, but when your son is kicking and screaming in the hotel room because you've said "Let's go to the candy store!", it's hard to rationalize. Not many people probably understand, but that's the way these kids are.

<u>Support</u>

We stayed overnight when we planned to meet with a support group of families, as well. Many of the other families seeing our therapist lived closer, so it made sense to meet there instead. I didn't actually think that I would want to take part in a support group. It seemed like a strange concept to me. I am not very outgoing, and was hesitant to take part. Our therapist highly encouraged it, and we met some other families. The first time we met, I was really nervous. The boys must have been, too, because they were displaying their anxiety behaviors (which onlookers would view as naughtiness). I felt kind of out of place at first, because I didn't have much in common with these families, aside from having a child with RAD and PTSD. I, however, am one of the few families to have 2, and the only single parent. Their kids were all much further along in therapy. They had been seeing our therapist for a lot longer. Mine were obviously in need of therapy, and I was just as obviously in need of support. The boys acted out, but the parents didn't act like I was crazy. For the first time, I got the impression that others felt like the boys did need intervention. It was opposite to the interactions I was used to. These people understood. It was a relief to have that.

Once we began meeting with the other families, I almost craved that feeling of being understood- I looked forward to meeting up with these families. I finally could speak about what was really going on in our family, without having to hear the words "all kids do that". These people knew. They had stories of their own. They, too, had been down. They, too, saw the hurt in their children that no one else could see. They, too, had been hurt by their children, and suffered the heartbreak of loving children that did not have the capacity to reciprocate their love. It was so nice to know I wasn't the only one.

The people making up the support group are from all different cultures. There were some from rural areas, some from the city, some with children adopted from foreign countries, some with children adopted from foster care, and others with biological children suffering from RAD, as well. The religious beliefs varied greatly, too. A Mennonite family that we met during the first get-together has been very supportive throughout our healing process. All of us had come together with the same problem, regardless of our beliefs, financial state, marriage situation, profession, or education. We all were wanting the same thing- to heal our children and ease their pain. It is a great unifying factor. Most of the time, the support group meetings have been wonderful.

There was one incident where a family hosted the others, and this particular family had already completed therapy. The other children in the house included a boy about the same age as James. This child was, according to most people, "normal". He had all of the normal boy toys. Toy swords. Nerf guns. Nerf guns and toy swords are not exactly safe for my children. This was the second time we'd been to this home, but the first time we went, I had brought James his own stuff to play with- he was not to touch anyone else's stuff.

The previous support group meeting, at a different home, I had brought the boys some coloring books and crayons. There were plenty to share. I didn't know what to expect at that home the first time, so I was trying to be prepared. Another child asked James to share that time, and he had ignored him as he requested several times. I encouraged James to answer the child, but regretted it almost immediately when he verbalized clearly that he wasn't going to share. The other families, thankfully, were not looking down upon me or my child. I asked Jackson to share, and he did so, very willingly. So, that is why the next time we met, James was only permitted to have the book I had him bring, and nothing else. He didn't have to share, but he was not permitted to play with anyone else's stuff. The second time we went to this home, I had agreed to allow him to try again to play with others. I regretted it within seconds. He immediately went for all of the things that I do not allow. He was not cautious of anyone, and actually sought out people to "shoot" with the nerf guns- other parents. He did not listen to anything I said, and actually disappeared somewhere in the home for several minutes. An aquarium nearly met its doom during a swordfight. Jackson was upset because the older boys were being so mean to him, and he got downhearted when he accidentally ran a vehicle into a baby. I was a wreck. Another family also had a child about the same age as James, and the similarities were alarming. One difference, however, was that their child responded to their requests to come to them, or to stop engaging in certain behaviors. James just didn't do that. We finally left, and when I said that they couldn't play their tablets, they had a fit, but were asleep within 5 minutes. All of that naughtiness must have been exhausting. They finally felt comfortable enough to sleep in the car, which was a big step. Initially, it was extremely rare for either of the boys to fall asleep while riding in the car. I found that odd, since all of my sister's kids would go to sleep in the car all of the time.

The support group, for the most part, was extremely helpful. Despite my hesitation and perception of what it would be like, it felt good to know that others were dealing with the same kind of problems, and could offer support in a way that no one else could. They had dealt with not being understood by the public, or by close family members. They had seen the hurt in their children. These people could relate to our daily lives. It was a big part of getting through the tough times.

One weekend, when we were killing time to be able to meet up with some other families, it was kind of a dreary day, and we decided to just stay in our hotel room and watch TV until check-out time. We were all quiet and comfortable, a rarity at that time. I had brought juice boxes, fruit, yogurt, and cereal bars for breakfast since this particular hotel didn't serve a free breakfast, and minimizing public settings is always wise. We'd eaten, and were just hanging out. Jackson asked if he could have another cereal bar. He took one out of the box, held it up, and asked with nice manners. I thought for a second, and thought "Why not?" I didn't know how much he'd actually eat when we were visiting with the other families, as often neither of the boys would eat *anything* at those events. I said "yes". He said "Actually, I don't want it." I said- "Why don't you go ahead and eat it- I'm not sure how long we'll have to wait to eat lunch." I was startled to hear the scream, and the angry words that came next. He said, "I don't want it. I don't like that kind. I'm not eating it!" My head was spinning. I played back the conversation in my head. He asked for the cereal bar. I said yes. He had a fit. What was wrong with this picture? Who has a fit when someone says yes? Only my defiant son. It's almost funny, now. Who would believe it? A child becoming upset when he asks for something and is told yes. That's not normal for most kids. It was, however, normal for us.

On the Way

Driving home after therapy instead of staying overnight wasn't much better. The days we'd drive back home were long and hard. We'd leave at noon from work to get to our appointment by 2:00. We'd have therapy until 5:00 or 6:00, grab fast food, and return home. There is a place near the therapist's office that serves ice cream sandwiches with the kid's meals. It was our typical choice for the way back. I'd put the ice cream in the cooler, and they'd eat pretty quickly to get to their ice cream. Jackson is the kind of kid who likes to be neat and clean. He does not like to be sticky.

On one memorable occasion, he was dawdling while eating the ice cream. He was becoming irate as the ice cream began to melt. While he was throwing his head back and screaming, the ice cream, of course, continued to melt. This only made him even more distressed, and he increased the volume and pitch of his screams. He started to get rather violent at this point, and was kicking and rocking in his car seat. I warned him. I told him that if he didn't stop, I was going to take his ice cream away. He wouldn't have to worry about it dripping on him if I took it. He didn't want to hear anything I said, not that he could over the sound of his own screams. He was absolutely out of control. The "I hate you face" was very much present. I couldn't take the screaming any more. I pulled over and threw that ice cream sandwich out the car door. His initial shock was replaced with complete rage in a matter of about one second. He grabbed the Styrofoam cup to throw it at me, but he was so angry that he crushed it when he grabbed it. His cold drink splashed out all over, with the majority of it going right in his lap. He was so mad that he clenched his little fists and shook with anger. He started screaming "I'm wet, I'm wet!" After a minute or so of anger, he resigned himself to sadness, and I gave him paper towels to attempt to dry some of the mess, and we threw the ice cubes out on the side of the road. He sadly cried for a while, but recovered before we got home.

Another trip home, this time after we'd stayed the night and were heading home the next day, I created the perfect opportunity for the children to distrust me. One of the towns on the trip to therapy had an ice cream shop. I remembered from when my brother had played ball there many years before. I never imagined that it might have been gone. I told them about my plan only minutes prior, so as not to endure a fit that would prevent us from enjoying the treat. I turned towards the ice cream place, only to find the building with a large dumpster outside of it, and a sign telling about a new restaurant "Coming Soon". You can't possibly understand what it means to disappoint children like these. I said we'd stop in the next town, close to home and get some ice cream. I tried to compromise with having root beer floats at home. I came up with every possible comparable offer, but the fact remained: I had deceived them. I was no better than those "caregivers" before me. *They* never did what they said. *They* couldn't be trusted. I had no way of preventing this problem, really. What harm would stopping for ice cream be? It should have been fine. I still managed to get them an ice cream treat somewhere before heading home, and I am pretty sure we had root beer floats the next day, too. I followed through, but the emotions exploding in all of us after we found the place closed were not settled easily. They were feeling that same disappointment that they had felt before. I was a mess- feeling upset with myself for misleading them, angry that they couldn't get over it, and saddened that it seemed like the whole world was against us. It should have been fun to stop for ice cream, and even if "typical" kids would have thrown a fit, most would have been reassured by the alternatives provided. Mine were not. I could do nothing to alleviate that feeling of disappointment. What made the whole matter worse was the weekly visual reminder of the incident during the next several months. The highway was closed for construction, and the detour led us right past the closed ice cream shop as they transformed it into a sandwich shop. We witnessed the progress on a weekly basis, but had no interest in stopping for sandwiches. Ice cream, just that one time, would have been great.

The car trips were atrocious, because even if things were going as expected, Jackson was so bitter that he would find something to become upset over. I was becoming very desperate. I had started using children's music (mostly self-esteem boosting) in the car. There was one song that I had forgotten about for years. A Jim Cosgrove tune called "No More Cryin' Tonight" came up on the playlist, right in the middle of one of Jackson's fits. I could pretend that the timing was just perfect, but the fact was that Jackson was almost always screaming, so it was just a matter of time until the song came up. It became my new mantra. Whenever the fit would begin, I would skip to that song.

Every little thing is gonna be alright,
Every little thing is gonna be alright,
Every little thing is gonna be alright,
and there's no more cryin' tonight...

I would try to get him to sing it, to no avail. The lyrics almost seemed to be written just for us. I'm not quite sure if I ever would have been comfortable singing any other song in the same way, but the words were meaningful, and repeating that song, again and again, allowed me to keep driving. I needed to remain sane. I needed to get to wherever it was that we were going. Maybe it was similar to the way my boys' behaviors allow them to distance themselves and avoid "feeling" temporarily. Whatever the reason, I felt that the message was good, and it allowed me to continue on.

Walk with me, hand in hand,
We'll do the very best we can.
Together in strength, we'll take a stand,
And there's no more cryin' tonight.

Rest your weary head right here,
And together we'll talk away our fears.
With my hand, I'll wipe your tears,
'Cause there's no more cryin' tonight.

At first, he would just scream louder, and I'd turn up the volume. I hope I didn't damage my sons' hearing with the loud music I subjected them to, but in all fairness, Jackson's screams could still be heard over the music blaring from the speakers.

James, if he wasn't watching a video on the way back, I soon discovered, would become "carsick" after therapy. That long drive without distraction gave him too much time to think. It would even carry through to a Saturday drive back. Only once in the hotel did he have trouble, but I think it had more to do with a conversation we had as we went into the hotel. We were talking about missing a birthday party the next day (we were not up for birthday parties, even if we had been in town). He said

144

something about never having a birthday party. I reminded him that he had one just before I got them. He didn't remember, but seemed to want to know about it. I told him, and it must have stirred up something in his thoughts, and he got sick. We've been together for about 2 years, and the only time that child has thrown up is when there is anxiety or memories involved. He has only displayed allergy symptoms, never had a cold, and never even had to miss school other than for therapy or avoiding trauma triggers. I am grateful for his health, but it's truly amazing that the emotions can make him so sick, yet he fights off everything else.

Therapy was hard, but it was more for *my* benefit during those first several months. I needed to understand my kids, and they needed the support that I learned to provide. James would be ALL over the place while we were there. He would climb, touch things he shouldn't, roll on the floor- anything he shouldn't have been doing. Any act of aggression towards me was dealt with hastily. Our therapist set the limits on aggression very early on, and with little room for confusion. The boys would both test her, and me, time and time again. Jackson almost seemed as if he wanted to have a fit and be restrained. It seemed that he would push and push until intervention was required. He was absolutely the best at making me feel horrible, though. While he was needing to be held, he would call for me. "Help me!" "I NEED you!" "Please!" "I want you to let me go." "I want you!" The "I want you" would be the first cry after he had just pinched, hit, scratched or kicked me. He didn't really want me, he just wanted to exert his control over me. Our therapist told him like it was, and he didn't always want to hear that. He sure could make me feel bad, though. After he finally seemed calm and was released to me, he would start over by hitting me or squeezing my arm, only to be restrained again by the therapist. Therapy was exhausting. Some days, they would decide to have a fit when we

145

were walking out the door, ready to go. I guess they just weren't ready to leave, yet. I don't know what I expected therapy to be like, but that wasn't it. The progress was slow, and honestly, seeing the good during that time was not a possibility. Time gave me a much better perspective.

James and Jackson were experts at adding difficulty to every task. Every time we tried to do anything, it was always met with disaster. My dad required knee surgery that summer, and given that his large garden was already planted, my parents would need some help to keep it up. My mom and I were digging potatoes, and of course, enlisted the "help" of the boys. James gave up immediately, and his whines were constant. "It's too hard", and "I'll never find one... oh here's one! I'm good at finding potatoes." became just part of the background noise. It was lovely. Jackson was really being helpful. He would carry the potatoes to the wheelbarrow, and come back for more. James was stomping and pacing and bathing in negativity, for the most part. The "James Show" of sudden excitement would appear for only seconds before the "I can't attitude" returned for what seemed like a long time. It was typical for him.

My mom and I began the final search for potatoes, while Jackson began "counting" the potatoes and making a pile on the ground. I told him to put them back. I asked him to stop taking them out of the wheelbarrow, but he ignored me. We finally found all of the potatoes that we were going to find, and started to get things put away. I looked at Jackson, proudly standing beside a pile of probably 150-200 pounds of potatoes. I chuckled and said "That's great, but you better start putting those back!" He looked at me in shock and displayed his outstretched hands to say "what?!" After crossing his arms and stating, "I'm not doing it!", I knew we were in for a battle. I told my mom I'd be right back. I grabbed the sunscreen, and some water. I guess when he saw the sunscreen and bottles of water, he knew I meant business. He, however, was hot and tired, and did not care if I "meant business". He did not want to return all of those potatoes to the wheelbarrow. He ended up completing the job, even though I broke down and helped a little. It was hot and we were both very tired.

<u>Home</u>

That summer we survived, but barely. The house was finally ours in June, but the boys were not excited. They were nervous, and acted up at the final walk through, as expected. It had rained, and they ran through the house, tracking mud from one end of it to the other. They were wild and were trying to do flips (falling down, and screaming all the while). Then we went outside, and my unique children found a unique insect. We would find out later, after looking it up, that it was a click beetle. I had lived in that neighborhood for my whole life, and had never seen anything like it. It looked like a fishing lure- fake and plastic. I didn't think too much of the boys playing with it. When it clicked, I still thought that it might be a lure or a toy. Then Jackson picked it up again, and within seconds, he screamed in terror. The darn thing had somehow pinched or bitten him. He was screaming bloody murder, James was laughing and cackling, and the realtor was speechless. When she came up with something to say, I heard her explain that she didn't know what the thing was either, and was actually knowledgeable in entomology. I had a screaming 4 year old, and a 7 year old who was hysterically laughing and intent on catching that stupid bug.

I wanted to be done. I tried to take pictures of them putting the "sold" sign in the yard, and on our new front porch, but no pictures were happy or display-worthy. The realtor, I believe, was overjoyed to sell her first (or at least one of her first) homes. I had been her daughter's preschool teacher several years before, and I'm sure that I never looked as exasperated as I did that day. She, bless her heart, was another one of those "all kids do that" people. Yes, I'm sure that all kids would be overwhelmed and not exactly on their best behavior while "walking" (meaning running, skipping, jumping, stomping, climbing, rolling, pushing, leaping, or any other form of movement BESIDES walking) through their new home. Not all children manage to be injured from an unidentifiable insect, or break the railing of the new home on the porch- in more than one place, or stab each other with sticks from the yard, or cover the entire house, including the beige carpet, with mud. They really don't.

The realtor gave me a gift the next day when I signed the final papers. It contained a nice children's book, Band-Aids, antibiotic cream, and a cute little picture frame. When I got to the last two items, I laughed like I hadn't in a very long time. She had also given us insect bite cream, and headache medicine. It was funny. The thought of that gift makes me smile even today.

We moved in as quickly as possible, and honestly the transition itself shouldn't have been too difficult. It was only two very tiny blocks away from my parents' house. We kept the same routine with supper together, for convenience as well as consistency. I also was not capable of doing much while the kids were awake, and fixing supper was beyond my maximum out-of-hand's reach time of 30 seconds. I was doing all required tasks of setting up and maintaining the house after the boys were in bed, asleep. They could not handle much of anything. Even watching TV could turn dangerous very quickly. I was grateful to have other adults around during any type of meal preparation. The boys hated our new house. I wanted so badly for them to finally be happy. I thought that it might help them feel better about things.

149

I thought they would realize that our family really was forever, and that the house was OURS. The house only created more opportunities to express fear. At the time I'm writing this, it has not improved greatly, either, even after a year in our home. I thought that it was just the basement, at first. It is not fully finished, but has sheetrock walls and adequate lighting, even if it is ugly. I put white baseboards on, and painted the walls a sunny pale yellow. James even expressed to the therapist that I had done that so he wouldn't be scared, but it did nothing to ease his fears. So we have all of the toys upstairs instead, even though the basement would be ideal.

When we moved in, money was fairly tight, but not as tight as it would eventually get. Our therapist suggested separate rooms (there is still the chance that James might attack Jackson), but there are only two bedrooms upstairs, so the boys must still share a room. Since safety is always my highest priority, the camera was set up before they slept in their new room. The bedroom is fairly narrow, but has sufficient length. I had considered moving the bunk bed I'd purchased for my parents' home, but the layout of the room, and the assembly complications influenced my decision to look for other options. In the midst of the rabbit attack and other interruptions, I realized that I had put that bed together in the opposite direction it needed to be. Rather than try to disassemble the bunk bed and start over, I affixed the ladder (more permanently than intended) to the opposite side. I figured it might be nice to have a bed they were comfortable in at my parents' house, should an emergency arise, or if they became so emotionally secure that I could leave them to go out. It's not happened yet, but maybe someday.

I decided on an offset bunk bed for their new room, but couldn't find one available for purchase. I settled on custom-designing the bed for the boys to fit the room. Since school was starting, and money was tight, I couldn't do it until Christmas break. I worked really hard to design it, and changed it a few times.

The biggest problem with this plan was that I felt terrible having them sleep on mattresses on the floor for a few months. I kept thinking how horrible I was to give these boys a home where they didn't even have a bed. I rationalized that they hadn't been sleeping in beds before I got them, either. James slept on a couch or the floor, and Jackson had been sleeping on a table or the floor. They didn't know what sheets were. When my mom asked what they slept on when this knowledge came to light, James told her about the couch and said "it was scratchy". So I kept telling myself that it was fine, and that mattresses on the floor was still better than before, but I was disappointed in myself every day. I didn't even move my bed in until after they were sleeping in their new bed. I couldn't live with myself knowing that I was sleeping in a bed while I wasn't providing that for my kids. Regardless, we were in our new home, mattresses on the floor, but we were "home".

I must say that I'm still saddened by the way that they responded to the new house. I was so hopeful that they would really be pleased and content with the fact that we had our own home. I guess the best thing about it was that the fits were less stressful for me. I didn't have to worry about how my parents were feeling about listening to a screaming kid. It made it much easier. Except for Sunday mornings. A church is right across the street from our home.   They figured out that I did not like them making a scene as the church-goers were arriving. The favorite thing to do was to decide to get upset over something after breakfast. Then, as the folks began arriving, they would go to the door and scream "Stop, you're hurting me!" or "Let me go!" while I was across the room from them. Only one at a time would do this, but typically it was James. How he could pick this particular time of the week to do this still amazes me. I used to think this kind of thing was just a matter of coincidence. If you have kids like mine, you'll realize, too, that it just isn't the case. There is no such thing as coincidence when dealing with kids like these.

James and Jackson didn't necessarily act out any worse as we moved into the house, it's just that they seemed scared of absolutely everything. They still act that way today, nearly two years after we became a family. I was super excited about the house in so many ways. It had a nice yard, completely fenced in, which was a big selling point! For children without boundaries, fences are a must. It came with a decent playset that was right outside the kitchen window. I liked it. The first thing I realized about the yard was the fact that even fences do not provide sufficient boundary markers for my children. The second thing was the reminder that my children couldn't play. I filled the sandbox in the playset, tightened the bolts, and shared my excitement about having such an ideal yard to play in. They were less than pleased. They acted as if playing in the sandbox was pure torture. The playset that I thought was safe was viewed much differently after my boys demonstrated their "play" while using it. The rope was the first thing to have to go. The fence was no more a boundary than a line in the dirt. Somehow, even though our new roof was very high, balls would "accidentally" go on top. How a window wasn't broken the first week, I'll never know. The railing on the porch was not very secure (as they had proven so plainly before the house was even ours). They simply could not handle staying away from it. They were not able to play anywhere as I tried to get moved in. I took a couple of afternoons while they were at daycare, before my school year started, to get moved in. I left my rabbit at my parents' house until I could get another camera set up to keep him safe. Finally, somehow, we began to get settled.

The fits were so much less nerve-wracking for me without having my parents as an audience. The other contributing factor to the fits becoming less overwhelming was a result of our therapist's suggestion. Jackson would get really upset when James would have a fit. It scared him a lot, and he felt sorry for James. He couldn't stay away, but he couldn't stick around either. It was really hard to deal with him coming and going out of the room, and he was so unhappy, too. The therapist suggested that Jackson get a "party bag" of stuff that he could have to distract him when James would have a fit. He'd get a treat (like fruit snacks or candy) and a toy or video that would keep him happy for a little while, and I could tend to James. That was the turning point for James and his fits. James would get even more upset, at first, but his success at making Jackson's life miserable was at stake. He couldn't let Jackson be happy at his expense. It didn't take long until James decided that many fits per day were making Jackson too happy. He didn't stop them, by any means, but the frequency was certainly diminished. The final straw was when Jackson was provided with a toy that belonged to James when a big fit would start and Jackson had been targeted. James would have no part of that. It took a while, but he eventually decided that the fits weren't worth it. They became less severe and finally, a rarity.

What's a Vacation?

Our existence was tremendously stressful. This was about the time of year that the former grandmother had come to take Jackson, and I believe he was reacting to memories of that event. He began to rub tags again, to soothe himself. I felt really guilty cutting out all of the tags from his shirts, but I didn't like to see him with his hand up his shirt constantly. I finally came up with the idea to sew the tags in the front pocket of his pants. This solved our problem. He could still rub the tags, and it was no longer obvious to anyone. So now, I added "tag-sewing" to my to-do list for every new pair of pants. No matter what I tried, however, our days began and ended with conflict. The boys made everything difficult, and I was still struggling to figure out how to adapt to their methods of disruption. We had NO fun. I felt like all we ever did was try to survive, which is really pretty accurate at the time.

I think that I must have been insane, but I decided that we would take a little trip. We hadn't gone on any type of vacation since our overnight stay from "Santa". Our therapist was taking her vacation just after Labor Day. I thought that would be a good time to do something. I wasn't wanting to do anything huge- just go to a zoo in Omaha, which is about 3 hours away. I had learned from experience that letting the kids know anything in advance wasn't helpful to prepare them, it just gave them opportunity to sabotage the event. I picked them up at the same time we usually went to therapy, on Friday. When we started to go the opposite direction on the highway, James figured out that we were not going to therapy. I was kind of excited, and nervous. I told them what we were doing, and James reacted positively, which was a surprise. He was really excited and happy after letting the idea sink in. I would find out later, through his writing work from school that he had a big lump in his throat from anxiety when he thought we were going to therapy that day, and being able to avoid therapy that day was a relief for him. Jackson, however, did not take the change of plans well. His screaming in the car, at that time, wasn't an everyday occurrence anymore. He decided to bring that high-pitched, blood curdling scream back into play, just for our "vacation". It isn't that far to the Nebraska border from our home, but it was a *very* long drive that day. He was so upset. He didn't say that he necessarily wanted to *go* to therapy- I think it was just the concept of change.

Preparing him wouldn't have helped, however. We'd tried that route for things, and he would do things to ruin the plans before we'd even gone. Once we got to the state line, I pulled over the car. We were right in front of the "Welcome to Nebraska" sign. If we had been a "normal" family, pulling over at that time, it would have been a wonderful photo opportunity. Needless to say, a screaming 4 year old and a fed-up 7 year old weren't exactly photogenic right then.

I probably yelled. I know I shouldn't have. I knew that he had a hard time with EVERYTHING. I also had just been crushed, yet again. I was so excited to take my kids on their first "vacation". We were staying two nights at a hotel. That was a first for them. I was pleased that James had reacted positively, although he was asking a million irrelevant questions to tame his anxiety. No questions related to our trip, just his usual "How old are you?",

"What if the sky was green?" kind of questions. I thought that Jackson would be upset initially, but I really believed that he would have come around before we'd driven that far. I was already exhausted and overwhelmed, and we hadn't left the state yet! I told him that he better knock it off, or we would just turn back around and not go on vacation. I asked him if he knew what vacation meant (not very nicely, I'm sure). He said "no", and I explained that it was a trip- just for fun. We would stay at a hotel, just like when we went to therapy, and we would come back on Sunday. I don't think he thought we were coming back. I am not really sure, because he can play dumb almost as well as James can. Regardless, I said that screaming in Nebraska was not going to be allowed. If he wanted to come have fun with us, then he needed to *stop that screaming*. He didn't suddenly transform into a lovable happy child, but the screaming became less shrill and almost stopped.

He figured out a new way to make things difficult. He said he had to go to the bathroom. Maybe he really did have to go, who knows? He was letting me know about it, leaving no doubt that there was a great sense of urgency. We stopped at a town, and he ran off in the parking lot where we stopped. I got after him about it, and made sure to turn on the child lock on his door again. I held his hand as we walked in. He twisted and pulled the whole way, making enough noise to turn heads. At least there wasn't anyone I knew there. It was only strangers thinking I was squeezing my 4 year old's hand with enough force to break his little fingers. The way he carried on, I know that's the way it looked. A longer walk, and I just might have started to!

We got back in the car for the final leg of the trip. The first thing I planned to do with them was something my dad had suggested. There is a foot bridge over the river that forms the boundary between Iowa and Nebraska. I had been practicing for a couple of weeks with them, working to get them to ride their scooters to a certain point (a tree, a sign, a house, a break in the sidewalk), and stop. They had been doing fairly well, so I had packed their scooters and helmets for the walk over the river. I can't say as they followed directions very well that day, but it could have been worse. They almost ran a biker off of the path, and nearly were hit by another. It really could have been worse, though. The line is marked for the Iowa/Nebraska border, and I took pictures of them jumping over it, and standing with one foot in each state. They looked happy at the moment. We went all the way over to the other side, and started our return. There were signs to read, and there were some pennies on the beams supporting the bridge. They asked about them, and I said that it was probably people making wishes. I dug out a few pennies, and they made their wishes. I wished for us to survive the trip- but I should have made it clear that survival wasn't enough- being happy was the fantasy I really desired. James didn't tell me his wish, but before we completely crossed the bridge, Jackson shared his. He said "I wished you would go away". I knew, already, that closeness was scary for him, but that was pretty blunt. Although I was hurt, I honestly let it go, and had forgotten about it until he reminded me of it about 5 months later. It took me a minute when he shared about that memory to figure out what he was talking about. His random statement was simply "Remember when we were on that bridge, and I wished you weren't around anymore?" I know people always say "all kids do that," when I say what my kids have done, but I don't know any 4 year olds that wish their mother away, then *remember* that wish five months later.

Anyway, as for the trip, the next stop was the hotel, and they did their typical off the wall, outright horrid check-in routine. They ran off, climbed on the counter, hung on it, and then decided to hit each other. One would start crying, then sought vengeance. The other would let out a scream, and the first victim/second perpetrator would start laughing, which started the cycle all over again. All this while I tried to fill out the forms and remember our license tag number. I gave a 5 minute lecture before checking in at any hotel, but it never worked. After we finally got checked in, we went up to the room. I gave another pointless lecture about behavior. What a joke that was!

We went to a restaurant to eat, which was an unpleasant adventure, too. Jackson was overtired, as he didn't sleep in the car. He was super whiny and grouchy. James was displaying his obnoxious anxiety behaviors, and making a scene. The service wasn't exactly the best at the restaurant, but that wasn't the worst of the problems. I remember drinks being spilled, James on the floor under the table picking up pennies he found, and Jackson crying because he wanted a penny. Then, despite my repeated requests for James to stay in his seat, he jumped up from under the table as a waitress walked by carrying a tray. It of course, fell to the ground, and James laughed. I apologized, and I'm sure I looked like a fool. The boys had refused to eat, but made a big mess. I left a decent tip, despite the poor service, and couldn't get back to the hotel fast enough. Then we had fits over taking a bath, sleeping arrangements, and I even had to do the hand-over-the-mouth task to get the screaming to stop. Jackson had figured out how to bite me during those times, so it was equally unpleasant for me.

I called my mom in tears, hoping that the boys were actually asleep, not just faking. I was so upset. I had looked forward to this trip with so much excitement and optimism. I knew that I shouldn't get my hopes up like that, but I kept setting myself up for disappointment. I was disgusted with myself for not knowing better than that, and discouraged that my kids really couldn't have a good time or even begin to enjoy anything special. I actually considered driving back that night or first thing in the morning. There aren't words to describe the hopelessness I felt at that point. I was heartbroken. My poor mother didn't know what to say. There wasn't anything she could have said to make things better, but listening to me was the best thing anyway. I needed to vent. I managed through the night, and decided to go ahead and try the zoo.

That day was honestly one of our best together. There were a few setbacks here and there, but overall it was a great day. We were all tired, of course, by the end. Our difficulties were minor compared to our typical struggles, however. Jackson had decided once, about midday, that he wasn't going to leave one of the exhibits. He ended up coming, but it wasn't without making a bit of a scene first. James had a fit because he wanted to spend his money at one of the little gift shops, but I said that he should wait for the main one as we left. They were not pleased when I insisted that they eat and drink, but they complied without a big scene. The only other issue during our time at the zoo was the prairie dog encounter. I couldn't get Jackson to leave things on the ground at all. He picked up an acorn or something, and threw it toward one of the free-range prairie dogs. The little prairie dog thought that Jackson was feeding him, and came up closer. For a quick moment, there was a cute scene. Jackson was bent over, talking to the prairie dog. He had his little backpack on (I had them both wear backpacks "for snacks", but the real reason was because the handles were quite helpful when one needed to be retrieved or held on to). Then the prairie dog went after his shoelace and wouldn't let go! Jackson actually ran to me, which was awesome, but the fear in his eyes was not a pretty sight. To top it all off, the poor little guy couldn't say blend sounds accurately, so when he spoke of the encounter, it was a "fairy dog" that attacked him. Despite the guilt I have from finding the whole matter amusing, I can't help but laugh out loud at the thought of it, even now. He wasn't hurt, but he still talks about that "fairy dog attack".

After the zoo, we went to a burger chain that had a bunch of apes and monkey statues outside of it. Jackson, after I got him out of the car, once again escaped death in a parking lot, even though he ran right through it to get a closer look at those statues. It must have scared him when he saw my terrified face, because even though he was not happy about anything at the moment, he was compliant when we went in to order our food. I needed to go to Wal-Mart for a forgotten item, where I discovered that Nebraska has liquor in their Wal-Mart. I didn't care if I looked like an alcoholic at that point. I had my 4 year old stuffed in the seat part of the cart, and my 7 year old in the back- right among the bottles of wine and liquor. I did get some funny looks, but it was a good buy for that wine, and they had my favorite kind! I enjoyed a bottle of hard lemonade when we returned to the hotel, and we finished our day without serious complications.

I should have just headed home that morning, probably. I pushed my luck, however. I found that there were boat tours that went under the pedestrian bridge we had walked over. I thought it would be neat and memorable to go on the boat tour to see the bridge that we had been on, and the other sights along the river. A new experience, for sure. Yes- a new experience- one of those things that were destined for misery. Actually, though, after the initial tantrums ceased, and we managed to board the boat, they seemed to enjoy it. It was just another hotel room scream-fest, and pouting performance prior to the event. James was the worst one that time. I'm not sure why he thought it would be so unpleasant. I was excited. It was a new experience for me, too. We made it through, and our only other planned stop before arriving at home was at a park for a picnic. They played a little, but at that time, playing was still not something they knew how to do. Jackson must have still been uncomfortable and irritable, because he insisted on wearing his baseball cap crooked. He is borderline obsessive-compulsive about things- needing them straight and clean. He was only wearing it that way to be obstinate. I wanted pictures, and I set it straight once. He promptly re-set it at an angle with a devilish grin barely showing in the corners of his mouth. He felt that it was worth it to sacrifice his comfort for the chance to make things unpleasant for me.

School and Life

School had started again, and James was doing very well in his new school, and his teacher was extremely sympathetic to his needs. To a fault. I had gone in before school started, and made a fool of myself explaining his unique needs, and providing safety information, since he needed to be protected from the former grandmother. They took everything in, and I explained that he might tell stories, and is likely to pretend to be incapable of doing things. He had actually pretended to be an incapable reader for almost the entirety of the previous school year. I let them know about his toileting and eating issues, and that he would be gone for therapy every Friday afternoon. They listened, but it wasn't long before James convinced them that he was perfectly fine.

A month or so into the school year, though, homework had become the battle that James chose to cause constant tension. He refused, he screamed, and he had those dying cow fits. He would "forget" how to hold a pencil. He spent hours upon hours avoiding the task that he could complete easily in less than five minutes. I asked the therapist what to do. She said that he should take care of it, and asked about anything the school had set up for him to do it with them, since he refused at home. There was a "homework club" that met before school every day, so I told her that I would bring him to that. The teacher was absent the first day, so James quit having a tantrum before too many people saw him.

The next day, he decided he absolutely was *not* going to go. I didn't give him the choice. We pulled up to the school, and I parked. He refused to get out of the car. Normally, getting him out of the car would have been somewhat easier, but circumstances made it harder for me to simply pull him out. A deer had run into our car over the weekend, and the car shop couldn't take it in until later in the week. The car door would only open from the inside. I reached in to open it, and James shut it again. I reached in again, while trying to hold the door open, and he tried to shut it on my arm. I finally got the door to stay open, pried his hands off of the seatbelt buckle, and then removed him from the car while he was still clutching the booster seat. I sat him in the grass, trying to avoid eye contact with the gawkers as they drove past. I pried the booster from his fingers, tossed it back in the car, and grabbed his backpack. He was lying, moaning, in the grass, stiff as a board. I said "Let's go". He continued his moaning. I said "You can walk, or I will carry you. You *are* going to school." I carried that 7 year old boy, dead weight, to the school door. The principal met us at the door. Immediately, my son, who never sheds a tear, turned on some fake crying. The "poor baby" comments began to start. "What's the matter, honey?" came next. I explained that he chose not to do his homework, and I brought him to work on it at the homework club. I was red in the face, I'm sure, and panting from the exertion required to drag a 7 year old boy out of a damaged vehicle, and carry him in, stiffly. I was mortified. He was led off by the principal, going out of her way to console that "poor child".

I didn't see his classroom teacher, but knew word would get around. At the parent/teacher conference that was already set for the following week, I brought up the homework issue. She, of course, had heard about the trouble we'd had when I tried to take

163

him to homework club. It was quite the sight, and the stories told, I'm sure, clearly depicted me as the "angry mom". I explained the problem, and the teacher told James that it was OK if he just did the reading for the homework, without completing the writing portion. I was not thrilled with that idea, but that's the way it went. I didn't like that he got out of doing the homework that he was fully capable of doing, but I was also relieved that we didn't have to spend the entire evening and every weekend battling over homework.

Other than the discussing the homework issue, the rest of the conference was occupied with statements about how wonderful James was. "He is so bright, and such a good student. I just love him! We don't have any problems with him,"--- which I interpreted as: "You are a crazy mom! There is nothing wrong with this child! You must be the problem." I was, and still am, very grateful for that teacher, however. James had a wonderful year at school. She had no idea about what was going on with him, but she is a very good teacher, and the structure and calm atmosphere was what James needed. The over-the-top effort she gave to guarantee his success *was* what he needed. Sometimes it frustrated me that he seemed to "get away" with not doing what he was perfectly capable of doing, but it was better than dealing with the challenges that would have come from trying to get him to do those tasks. Our therapist was right again. She said that preventing James from using homework as a tool to push us apart was the main goal. It was much nicer when we didn't have that problem anymore.

We had enough other problems, anyway. One of the most frustrating issues we dealt with was one that made me re-think the term "positive reinforcement". My children could not handle being told anything positive. I could say "That looks really nice!" only to have whatever it was be destroyed before my eyes. I might say- "Wow, you've stayed at the table for supper tonight," and expect the child to leave at the mention of it. He (either child) might kick me or throw food on the way, too.

The other issue with positive reinforcement was even more troubling. I would say something positive, without the intent to start any trouble, but no matter what I said, trouble followed. It might be something as insignificant as "thanks for shutting the door." It could be said to either child, and the other child would immediately go into a terrible fit, claiming "I never shut the door. You only like him." I couldn't say something like "You were fast getting your shoes on today!" without suffering negative consequences because the other child would suddenly have a fit as if I had just criticized him. This was a difficult time for me. I had always tried to be positive. Paying attention to little things, and giving positive feedback usually worked for me in the classroom. My sons did not respond the same way. I found myself stopping mid-statement when I was about to say something, and discovered that I had been conditioned for negativity. The boys didn't do that with malicious intent, but it had happened. It was almost like they *wanted* me to be negative. The life we led during that time was so difficult. I forced myself to continue on with my attempts at positivity. I held my breath after every statement, and eventually things became calmer. It wouldn't be soon, it wouldn't be easy, and I repeated the phrase "I love you anyway," more times than I can count. I honestly believe that they perceived any positive comment for one as hurtful to the other. The child not spoken to seemed to feel as if I had just intentionally insulted him. Jackson was the one who started the behavior, but James kept up with it longer. I think James really felt that anything I said positive to Jackson was an attack on him. I couldn't win. I struggled with maintaining positivity, and don't know how we made it through that time. I felt like there was no way out. I couldn't say anything positive or negative without being met with extreme displeasure.

I was beginning to feel a bit deflated at this point. I couldn't seem to do anything right, and the boys weren't happy. They took pleasure in my pain, and went out of their way to make sure that I knew it. Many of the behaviors they exhibited could be funny once, or even twice. Every day was a bit much.

The playing dumb was aggravating, but I almost preferred it to the other behavior of making *me* feel dumb. Jackson was an expert at making me start talking really loud at the store. I would say something- usually something insignificant. I might say "Let's go to get some strawberries." Jackson would say "What?" I would repeat myself, and then hear "What?" again. I don't know why, but I fell for it every time. I would catch myself shouting, only to look down and see Jackson trying not to smile. He was *good*. That was rarely the end of it, however. James would usually start to repeat what I had said, only to have Jackson say "What?" again. Then, knowing exactly what he was doing, James would use his loudest voice, pretend to be angry that Jackson wasn't "listening", and repeat my phrase. Then the physical fight would start, right in the back of the cart. Not only had I drawn attention to myself by talking loudly and pushing around my too-large-to-ride children in a cart, but I also had a shouting and poking match going on in the cart. My items would be redistributed and squashed, and I was left only with frustration. I always tried to talk with them later about what had happened, but I wasn't ever successful. I was just a part of their game. I felt bad thinking so at the time, but I now realize that even though their attempt to cause me difficulty was intentional, it wasn't with malice. Life wasn't safe, and the norm for them had been chaos. People weren't supposed to love each other, care about each other, or stick around. I was being tested, and even though I felt like I had been pushed to the limit, I must have had more strength than I realized. I *was* being manipulated by two very little boys. I admit it. I wish I could have been able to figure out the "right" thing to do at that time, but I really don't think there is one. I used every tool the therapist gave me, I read books, and I tried to keep ahead of them. I think that's all I could have done. Time and persistence with love and patience (all that I had, anyway) was the remedy. I wasn't completely ready to accept the idea of that during our difficult periods, however.

The only thing that Jackson and James could manage to do together was make things challenging for me. They teamed up for that fairly well. The hotel check-in routine was driving me crazy. I tried everything I could think of to bribe or threaten with, but it never worked. I told them that I would only take them swimming if they behaved during check-in, and even when I followed through, the following week was just the same. The therapist finally gave me the solution to my problem. I was to tell the boys "Please, act very naughty while I'm checking in today. I am really tired, and I don't want to take you swimming. Go ahead and run around and mess with the lamp like you usually do. Climb on the furniture and hit each other. I am too tired to go swimming, and I just want to go to bed." I didn't say it too realistically, but I wasn't laughing. I just said it to them, and walked on. They walked beside me, waited patiently, and didn't even fight over pushing buttons on the elevator. I smiled to myself, listening to Jackson whisper to James, "Be really good so she has to take us swimming." I was happy about the easy check-in. After I'd let it sink in a while, I realized that they controlled their behavior, just to spite me. Maybe they know that I was kidding all along, but it's still the only method I have for a good check-in process that actually works. It's odd to think about, but even if it means providing them with an opportunity to playfully get me to do something, my problem is solved. This simple concept made life so much easier. My check-in stress was gone. It was well worth it.

<u>Love</u>

The "dying cow" fits from James were still common for us. He almost seemed proud to be referred to in that way. I was becoming pretty desperate for progress. I still didn't quite grasp that love was foreign to them, especially James. I just wanted to do anything and everything I could to help them get better.

James is a sensory seeker, and I decided to try him out with a weighted vest. I didn't want to pay a fortune for one, and then have him refuse to wear it, so I decided to make my own. I went to my fabric box, and to my surprise, I had a good-sized piece of cow print fabric. I chuckled to myself, then put it back. I thought that I was being mean for even having the idea of using that one. Then I saw the solid black fabric, and picked both of them up. I decided to make it a reversible vest, with one cow-print side, and one solid black. That way he could just put the cow print on the inside, and not even see it. I set to work. It didn't take too long, but I probably filled it with more sand than necessary for weight. I made pockets to put the sand in at the top, intending for him to be able to use it under part of his costume for Halloween. When I was finished, I presented him with it. To my surprise, (and I'm sure his, too) he loved it! He even liked that it was the cow print and wore it with that side visible. He must have worn it for days straight. It was the first step towards his acceptance of me. I was thrilled. He took many steps backwards later, but this was still progress. James actually liked something that *I* did for him. I can still picture him standing there in that cow print vest, grinning from ear to ear. I had to remind myself of that from time to time, as those moments were rare.

For a while that fall, after the stress from memories of "Nana" coming the year prior subsided, Jackson was doing pretty well. His fits were diminishing, and he wasn't quite so demanding. The following month, I got my first "I love you" from him. It was 4 days before our year anniversary of the adoption. It was Halloween night, which happened to be on a Friday- therapy day. Even though the therapist is 2 hours away, our local high school happened to have a game in that city, on Halloween night. I had taken them to 2 different zoo trick-or-treat days with a friend of mine, promised them candy, and broke it to them that we weren't going trick-or-treating. They actually said they didn't want to, which was good, because James had developed irrational fears of anything and everything, and I was concerned about seeing frightening things while out on Halloween night. I dressed the boys up in uniforms to match our local high school football team, went to therapy, and then planned to meet my parents and my brother's family at the football game. We checked into the hotel after therapy, and were getting ready to go out to eat. Jackson was on this "I like you" kick. James was not doing his constant "hi" thing so much, and although Jackson's repetitive statement was a similar behavior, it was less frequent and more tolerable. It was actually nice to hear that he liked me. I was getting his shoulder pads ready to go, and helping him put on an extra layer of pants under his costume, because it was going to be very cold at the game. Once he was done, he walked over to the door, and said "I love you". I probably overreacted, but the words were so sweet and comforting to me that I was overcome with joy. I picked him up, and although he was now able to be held and

169

cuddled, the many layers and shoulder pads made it difficult to hold him as close as I wanted. I was elated. I had waited so long to hear those words, and I honestly think he genuinely meant it. James was immediately jealous, and stated "I like you", and gave me a hug that was much closer to being meaningful than in the past. He, too, had shoulder pads on, with the cow-print vest under that, so it is hard to tell anyway. He waited until we were in the elevator to tell me "I don't love you, though". I was too happy to be hurt by his statement at that time. I just told him that it was ok, I knew he would someday. I am so glad that Jackson's comment could build me up so much. I needed it, since James responded with "No, I won't."

We ate at a restaurant without any memorable difficulties, and the game went pretty well. I remember being very grateful that we had opted to avoid trick-or-treating, because there was a child with a mask on at the game that scared James a lot. Trick-or-treating could have been disastrous.

We celebrated adoption day, which happened to fall on picture day again. I still don't have any quality pictures of the two of them together. I actually purchased some of the horrible ones, just for kicks. They are so terrible that it's comical. In one, James appears to be choking Jackson. In most of them, they just look ridiculous. James looks like he is ready to attack, gleefully. Jackson puts on a face of disgust, or opens his mouth and gives an odd, unhappy look. It's terrible. This time, though not shown in the photographs, they were un-decorating the fake tree, and throwing the props around- kicking and throwing the presents and oversized ornaments. Why they can't handle *any* kind of different situation, even in a familiar setting is beyond me, but it is still a challenge.

I was trying to make the most of adoption day, and give them something really great, something that might also help us as we worked to heal. James loves to jump in the foam pit at this gymnastics place we go to for our child care center field trips. He is a sensory-seeker, and I thought that having something similar would be a good thing for him. I thought it might give him a "big" way to get himself calm, or work out the aggression he had in an acceptable way. I used large foam mats to cushion the walls, and bought tons of dense foam. I cut it into large cubes and placed it inside a cover. I was so excited about having a large jumping pillow right there in our house. My excitement was soon replaced with the all-too-common disappointment. They didn't seem to care about it at all. I knew that it wouldn't likely be something that Jackson would use to self-regulate, but I thought he'd really enjoy it- just to jump for fun. They jumped on it about 3 times, that same day, and never have touched it since. So much for my brilliant ideas.

More Mistakes

I was attempting to find opportunities to visit their birthmother, but having someone else watch the boys was difficult. I left them with my mom the first time. She brought them out shopping, and to lunch, and the boys mentioned that they dropped chips on the floor and smashed them, and spilled pop. I left them with her at an indoor playground place another time, which was better, but they still acted up. I left them with a friend of mine, (one with some knowledge about my kids) at that same indoor facility, but I found out that another adult had to break up my children from attacking one another. The worst away-from-me experience was really, really bad. My friend had invited us to go and stay with her at this child-themed park with "cabins". It was about a half an hour away from where I needed to be to visit, but I thought we could make it work. The place had a bunch of children's activities. It had a jumping pillow, a playground, a corn maze, and optional events that they could choose to do. It sounded great.

When I arrived, I was disappointed to find that it wasn't like I'd been imagining. There weren't *real* cabins. The place was a campground, with a few modified campers as "cabins". I should have left then, and taken my children from there, but I was still not completely aware of the significance of their PTSD triggers. I didn't really think that *every* place with campers would trigger trauma for them. I went to visit, and came back to find James in his galloping fairy state. He was hyper and not listening at all. They'd gone on a "fire truck ride" which took them down every pathway through the campground. My poor babies. We planned to stay, but I should have left. We did the activities, cooked hot dogs and s'mores, and tried to settle the kids in for bed. The boys were put up in the main room with the couch-bed. This was the memory that was most upsetting to James, but he couldn't voice it. I was in a small bedroom just off of the main room, and when he was still awake at midnight, I asked if he'd rather sleep where I was. I put blankets on the floor beside the bed, and he curled up and went to sleep. The next day, the boys were still agitated. They opted out of showering, which I agreed to let go. There was a person in a bear suit that came around, and my boys tried to knock him over, pull his tail, and unzip the costume. We decided that we'd had enough "fun". It was time to go. The "cabin" was not as expected, but to most families, it would have been fine. We were *not* most families. Things for us could be problematic, even with the best of circumstances. I was so upset with myself for putting the boys in an environment that caused them such difficulty. My friend told me that Jackson was concerned the whole time about my return when I had left to visit the birthmother. He was worried that I wasn't coming back. I get angry at myself for doing that to them, even if it wasn't intentional. I realized that I needed to work harder to make sure that my choices didn't negatively impact the boys.

By Thanksgiving, things were a little better, although James had decided to keep up with the food control issues. Even though things were improving, I still lacked a lot of patience, and James had not relented on many of his food-related issues. I believe at this time, there were still the court problems hanging over my head, and I was stressed, as usual. James decided that he was not going to try anything to eat at all. I saved his plate for him, and brought it home. I told him he didn't have to eat it, but he wasn't getting anything else unless he *tried* what was on his plate. He screamed. He went into his dying cow fit. It went on, and on, and on. Two and a half hours later, he was still screaming at our table. I was past my limit for patience. I had tried to remind him that he'd tried, and liked, the foods before. I was only requesting that he take "tiny mouse bites" of the food. I was getting a little worried about the safety of the food on his plate, since the meat had been sitting out for quite some time. About the time I was trying to figure out what would be safe for him to eat, he started throwing out the insults and, with authority, stating that he was never going to eat any of it.

I should have been able to let the comments go. I should have been the grown-up. I should have been smarter, and avoided the shame from what my actions would bring. I, however, was not. I was tired. I was frustrated. I was out of party bags for Jackson. The moaning screams had gone on for so long that I was beginning to wonder how the issue was ever going to end. I considered putting the plate back in the refrigerator, minus the meat. I might have been on my way to do that when the final straw was set upon the camel's back. James had a way of putting up his hands to protect his body when I approached him, especially if we were in the midst of a fit. He had begun to stop that, and I'd expressed distress that he would think I would hit him like that. I told him it bothered me that he didn't trust me enough to know that I wouldn't harm him in that way. As I walked near him, he was either in such a primal part of his brain that his protective instincts took over, or he knew that it upset me, so he put on a great performance of displaying fear. I have no way of knowing what the intent was. He moaned, screamed, covered his face, and looked as if he were in a panic.

I made one of my most regrettable mistakes that evening. I had lost every ounce of patience I had, and in my moment of temporary insanity, decided that he WAS going to eat some of that food. He ended up with food all over him, and I had a mess of spit-out food and smeared mashed potatoes to clean up. It was probably only about 5 seconds of stupidity before I managed to see that I'd gone too far. The mess was already made, though. I had to tell him that I should have done the relaxation exercises from therapy, too. I should have used the right part of my brain, and that I was sorry. I cleaned up the mess, sent him to the bathtub, but told him that he was not getting any treats that evening. If he wanted something, he could eat an apple. He opted for nothing. I am not proud of my actions that day, and wish that I had been able to avoid letting myself get so upset. We were 6 months into therapy, and 1 year post adoption. I was learning how to do things better, but being able to understand the boys' behavior, and deal with it appropriately and with consistency, would only come with time. While I waited it out, and used every ounce of strength I had, I hope that I only caused minimal delay and damage during the process. It was a rough time.

<u>Christmas</u>

The holiday times are always stressful, and our 2nd Christmas together was no exception. They worried about a "Nana encounter" during our Christmas Program again, but thankfully, she didn't show. We were invited to the charity event at the church again, but I politely declined. If they remembered us from the year before, I'm sure they knew why we decided not to come. James had decided that he all he wanted for Christmas was dead animal parts. Yes, you read correctly- dead animal parts. The idiotic Tooth Fairy ran out of special coins when yet another tooth (that really wasn't ready to come out) was put under his pillow with the expectation of money in return. She usually left unique coins like silver dollars and half dollars. James had written to the Tooth Fairy, and expected a return note. Stupidity and craziness must have led the Tooth Fairy to "trade" the tooth with one from my puppy. My puppy- "given" to me about 2 months before I got the boys would become my parents' dog, since additional pets were not really a good idea in our home. The puppy required a baby tooth to be extracted because it hadn't come out on its own, and I remembered that the vet had put it in the bag with the receipt and the tags for her shots.

The Tooth Fairy started something awful. James was ecstatic over the tooth. Then a lady from work gave him a deer antler (which was promptly taken away due to aggressive acts with it). The deer antler spent a really long time in the trunk of the car. Anyway, with these wonderful animal parts, James decided that he just wanted to create a new animal from dead animal parts. I was disgusted. I was even more horrified when he decided that he wanted a rabbit head to create this thing. The head from a *rabbit*. My favorite animal. I realize that this idea may have evolved from the Tooth Fairy's crazy exchange of teeth, but I was pretty unhappy that my son had decided that dead animal parts would make good Christmas gifts. Needless to say, he was not presented with any carcasses, and when our therapist helped him understand that he needed a license to be a taxidermist, he backed off. He gave the appearance of being deterred when he found out that blood was involved, but I thought that was odd. Why wouldn't there be blood involved? How could he not have thought of that image? He certainly was NOT going to be indulged with animal parts for Christmas gifts.

I was pleased when Christmas morning was not nearly as disappointing as the year before. They appeared much more excited for their "second Christmas", as James called it. Choosing other people's gifts as favorites, while ignoring the ones I gave, was still the plan for them. Santa brought some of the things I thought they'd like best, and my mom, too. I didn't want them to push away the things they'd like the most. I knew that if the gifts came from me, they wouldn't touch them. I gave them a few things from me that I really thought they'd enjoy, but set back many to come from others, just so they would actually use and enjoy the gifts. They wouldn't eat anything I made, and they had an aversion to anything I did for them- even when they demanded it of me. They were difficult, to say the least. Jackson got a new pair of shoes for Christmas, and he must have thought Santa had brought them. I reminded him a few months later that *I* gave him those shoes when he was wearing them, since he'd mentioned Santa. He never wore them again, aside from the time I said to go put on old shoes since the yard was muddy.

The biggest happening over the Christmas break was the bed-building. I was finally going to give them the bedroom they deserved. I ordered special soft flooring, and designed a bed that was suited to their own needs. I had originally thought that I would have James on the top part of the bed, but after a lot of consideration, I realized he would probably like the "cave-like" part underneath. I was shocked when they agreed with me. I allowed for lots of storage, and each of them was to have shelves at the foot of his bed for his own "stuff". There was also a plan for space for their stuffed toys. I changed my plan as I began to finish it to allow for a small play space under the upper bunk. I liked it better, and the boys were thrilled. It was the first significant thing I think they actually liked that I did for them. It was certainly the first time they admitted it.

It only took 2 trips to the lumberyard, surprisingly, and the cost came in well under what I had budgeted. I had to borrow the childcare center van to pick up the lumber, but we made it work. I was just glad that the boys behaved reasonably well during our lumberyard visits. We were likely standing out anyway, given our mode of transportation. I had to move the saw indoors after the first day, as the temperature dropped and it became dangerously cold. There was sawdust from one end of the house to the other, and the living room was practically a lumberyard for a couple of days. It was hard, but by the end of Christmas break, the boys had a decent bedroom. It was something they actually liked. They also liked the fact that I had to keep them quiet and away from my work while I was building the bed. I let them do something that I NEVER let them do, but it kept them occupied the entire time. I felt guilty about them being forced to sit and watch TV, but they were overjoyed. It was the last time they will probably ever get to see "Power Rangers", but they watched

178

hours and hours of episodes for a good share of the break. I forced them to stop to do other things from time to time, but they were always ready to go back to watching those shows that I considered stupid and overly violent. James couldn't watch "Curious George" without running from the room in fear or having nightmares, but for some reason, "Power Rangers" was perfectly fine to him. I didn't like the plan, necessarily, but it worked. They enjoyed themselves, and I was able to provide them with an acceptable bedroom.

We had to go back to school too soon, but it was pleasant for a very short time. Jackson was the first to falter. I believe that he had just gotten too comfortable. He liked his bed, and he liked spending time at home, finally. Things were good. When things were good, Jackson had to make them bad. He went back on a fit-throwing spree, which wasn't a wonderful thing, since James was also liable to have a fit at any given time. We were better, no question about it. Having time between tantrums was nice. They still couldn't play together. They still couldn't handle anything good happening. They still weren't really happy.

New Year, New Ups, New Downs

As we began the new year, Jackson was having a few ups and downs, but overall things were pleasant. James was struggling, but not quite as badly as before. He began to go for longer stretches of time without soiling his pants, and started to use the bathroom on his own, without being told to. His fits were becoming less intense, and less distant. During the whole first year a fit wasn't just a temper tantrum for James. He would lie on the floor, lifeless, drooling like an infant. He was "gone". There was no way to reach him until he was ready to face the world again. No amount of talking, attempting to soothe, or distraction would bring him out of it any faster. It was very frustrating to me. If there was any response, it was a purely instinctive survival behavior. He would scream and cower as if I was going to beat him. I tried talking softly, inching my way closer to him, but he would always pull away and make himself into a ball in the corner, using his arms to protect himself. I would get so upset after a 20 minute attempt to work my way within an arm's length of him, only to have him retreat to the corner in a panic. I was hurt. On too many occasions, I left the room, saying "Fine! Just come out when you're ready!" It was usually a very long time, and never without some other assistance with transition.

Having my own son afraid of me was hard. Even taking into consideration the rare times I spanked him (a swat or two on a fully clothed bottom), I couldn't come to terms with the fact that he couldn't allow me to get close. When he was in a fit like that, I unintentionally contributed to his decision to distance himself further. I remember once, after he had started to get a little better, he got into one of his fits. He was already almost gone, but was still showing some anger, trying to damage something. He was not all the way into the primitive state of being- drooling, moaning, and staring off into space. I, being upset myself, and trying too hard to make things better, decided that I would "force" him into "relaxing". Yes, being in a normal state of mind, I know how senseless that sounds. However, at that time, it seemed like a good plan. I started trying to massage his arms. I had been successful with my niece and a few difficult students I'd tried it with. This only caused James to regress back to that infantile state. He was overwhelmed, and as I tried harder to make it work, I pinned him down- so I could start from his shoulders to work down to his fingers, as had been calming to others I'd tried it with. My body being on top of his was too much for him. He started making the animalistic sounds, rocking his body, and choking on his own saliva. Although I was determined to "make him relax", that was too much. Even in my state of mindlessness, I was able to recognize that it wasn't going to work. That was simply too much for him. I have no idea what happened to my little boy to make him struggle with coping to the extent he does, but it had to have been something horrid. I can't even think about him looking like that without becoming overcome with emotion. Here he was, at 6 and 7 years old, with less coping skills than a 6 month old baby. Honestly, the progress James made the first year and a half was hard to see. He rarely participated in therapy, he wouldn't try to do anything that was intended to help him relax. He had gotten so much better in many ways, but in so many others, the progress was overshadowed by the significant problems that were so obvious to see.

Things had started to go pretty well, or at least a lot better than before. It wasn't great, but there were at least a few moments at a time that we might have together without one or both of the boys having fits. There was no doubt that the boys needed therapy, though. After things settled down again after the "too-happy" time after the new bed was done, Jackson was doing fairly well. He had one night where he tossed and turned all night long. I saw it on the camera, which would become bright anytime there was movement. He didn't seem to be awake, so I let it go. I didn't want to go and bother him. When I went to wake them in the morning, Jackson said "I'm wet". His pull-up had leaked, and his bed was soaked. I was so upset with myself for not checking on him. I was disappointed that he couldn't trust me enough to tell me he needed clean sheets and a bath. Why would anyone spend the whole night uncomfortable? Jackson is very much a "neat and tidy" little boy. He had to have been absolutely miserable in that soaking, smelly bed. I just couldn't believe it. I kept trying to figure out what I could do to help him feel safe enough to allow me to care for him.

Another time when James had gotten himself into a fit, I was trying to help him through it, and providing the seemingly insignificant support that my presence gave. He had been upset over a situation that reminded him of a past trauma or scared him in another way. He had calmed to a state of baby-like behavior, stuffing himself into my lap, but not comfortably. It was a forced position, with elbows prodding my ribs and his body stiffly folded "pretending" to be a baby. There was no sense of comfort, security, or relaxation as we sat together.

As we talked, I intended to provide him with understanding and support. I told him I felt bad about the bad things that happened to him, and that he didn't deserve to feel this way. I told him that he was going to get better, and someday he wouldn't have all of the hurt inside him anymore. We'd had discussions about faith before, and although we didn't belong to a church, I worked to instill the beliefs and values that are part of a Christian family. The only religious experience he had cared to share from his first family was one I knew couldn't be erased easily. He had been told that he was bad, and he was going to hell. I felt that organized religious services would have been difficult for us at first, and I think that I made the right choice to keep our faith strong at home. His first experiences at church weren't what I felt he should carry on with. Our discussions had led to the determination that God had brought us together. I was taken aback when this particular evening's discussion led James to ask me "Why did God make me like this? Why did He do this to me?" I felt numb. I didn't know what to say, but before I could think of anything, I had already spoken. I said, "I don't know. I really don't. What I do know is that God gave me you, and He gave you me. We needed each other, and even though I don't think it's right that all of those bad things happened to you, I know that if they didn't, we wouldn't be together. For some reason, God had a plan. He must have known that you were strong. Even though you don't feel like it now, He must know that you are going to grow up to be strong and help others in some way. He must know that I'm the one to be here for you and help you heal. We were brought together, and now we just have to get through all of the hard stuff. I wish that all that bad stuff hadn't happened. It makes me so sad sometimes that I want to cry. When that happens, I try to think about how we are going to be so much better than we would have if this hadn't happened." I hope it was the right thing. The biggest concern I have is that James might come out with the idea that I'm happy about the bad things if it meant he could be my son. I worry about how he interprets what I say, but I can only hope that the message I intend to give is heard. I didn't like the thought of my son having to worry that he had done something to deserve the horrible circumstances that had led him to be hurt so badly. He couldn't have done anything to deserve it, and yet, he couldn't believe anything different.

The days of constant fits were over, at least most of the time. The difficulty had not yet disappeared. They were still incredibly demanding, and impossible to keep up with. They could not be left unsupervised for even a moment. Jackson's favorite game was to "accidentally" kick or throw his clothing while removing it. It had gone on top of the door, in every corner of the room, and into my face (his favorite target). There were consequences for this, but nothing seemed to faze him. He loved bath toys, but the joy from hitting me in the face with dirty underwear was worth more to him. Once, while I was getting pajamas out, he "accidentally" kicked a pair of pants into the bathtub, where James was finishing up. I heard the commotion from all of about 6 feet away in the bedroom which is adjacent to the bathroom. I, not more than 3 seconds after the initial cackling began, found James getting ready to throw the dripping pants across the room. They must have weighed 5 pounds then- they were the worst possible pants to have ended up in the tub. I said "Stop! You're getting water all over!" James, still laughing, said "OK", and dropped the sopping mess right onto the bathroom floor. The pool of water spread quickly. We (I) had a spectacular mess to clean up. After the boys were done cackling, and both baths were done, I was getting Jackson's head dried off more, as he likes to leave it wet when the time has come to need a haircut. It ends up looking horrible with uneven spikes coming out of all sides of his head. Anyway, I, still dealing with the mess, told them "I really don't like the clothes going all over, especially when we end up with pants in the tub." This statement, of course, was met with giggles and laughter. I said "I don't think anybody would find this mess very funny." Without so much as a second to ponder a response, Jackson said "My first mommy would have laughed." Now there are a couple of different ways I can interpret this statement. First, he could be referring to the memory that he had of naughty behavior being perceived as funny. The initial thought I had, though, was not that. I figured that he was implying that *I* should have been thinking it was funny, like she would have. I have no idea what his thoughts were when he made that statement, but it made me realize that he still had his first mom on his mind.

It's My Party, and I'll Cry If I Want

When Jackson's birthday rolled around again, James was already worried about being jealous before the birthday even came. I was glad that he actually acknowledged it. Jackson was sort of hesitant about the birthday. He was kind of excited, but more anxious. I should have known that it would be a disaster, just like most things I expected to be pleasant. I woke him up, saying "Good morning, birthday boy!" He immediately responded with "Don't call me that". OK. Got it. I realized then that the bear was not ready to start the day. He got up, got dressed, and asked his usual question about whether it was a school day. The response confirming that it was indeed a school day prompted the typical cries of distress. Then he asked whether it was a therapy day. The response being yes was usually met with eagerness, but not that day. Apparently any statement from me was destined to ignite Jackson's temper. Upon finishing breakfast and dressing, I had a couple of presents for him to open. I thought that every little boy needed a pair of cowboy boots. I had a toy and a pair of cowboy boots for him to open that morning, and was saving the rest until later. He had gotten a new toy the weekend prior- he'd spent Valentine money from my mom on a Ninja Turtle, and was holding the treasured toy in his hand as he attempted to unwrap the gift. I said to him that I thought it would be easier if he used both hands, and that he needed to hurry because we had to get to work. He begrudgingly put the toy down and unwrapped the present. The boots were not a hit. He was not happy. They hurt his feet, he said (whether they did, I'll never know). He opened the next present while I tried to rush him along. It was really time to leave. He hated the boots, and told me so. I was hurt. I had given James a pair, too, as a present even though it was Jackson's birthday. I knew the jealousy would be too much, and it is hard for any kid when it's someone else's birthday. James loved his boots, but didn't admit it until later. He, too, was disappointed that it wasn't a toy, I believe. Jackson did not ever admit that he might like the boots. I wasn't ready to give up on them, and said that we'd go to the boot store over the weekend, to see if we might be able to find a pair that felt comfortable. He seemed to settle, somewhat, but was not entirely pleased getting into the car.

We were already running late, and about half mile out of town (it's about a 15 minute drive to the town we go to for work and school), when he started screaming that he forgot his toy- the one I had encouraged him to put down to open the present. I don't mean screaming in a way that just describes loud crying- he was out of control, and it was all directed at me. It was MY fault, he declared. I forgot his toy. I made him leave it. I don't even know what all he said, but my limit had nearly been met. He had hated the gift that I thought he would love. He was angry and hateful through and through. James was slightly better at that moment, but any emotional control he had disappeared when I lost mine.

It got worse when my mom got upset, too. She rarely got after my kids, but upon witnessing the hurt that they were inflicting upon me, she expressed her displeasure. She was aware of how hard I had worked for the boys to be happy, and the high hopes that I had for Jackson to have a nice birthday. I had loaded the car, packed because we were staying the night, gotten the treat bags ready for his class, made his special monkey cupcakes, wrapped all of the gifts, and been so excited about those stupid boots! I was crushed, and she saw it. She loves the boys without question, but she was not willing to allow their hatefulness towards me go on without being addressed. It likely made no difference to the boys, having Grandma upset, too, but I felt validated in my emotional struggles. I knew that it wasn't just me being overly sensitive. These times were far from easy, and far from over.

The rest of the weekend was... difficult. We survived therapy, a Walmart trip to get some ice cream, and disappointment over getting the hotel that didn't have an indoor pool. I was actually more disappointed than the boys. I had gotten Jackson some really cool boats to play with in the pool, and thought we'd end up with that one. If you are experienced with difficult children, you'll understand why a ball (which can reach the ceiling and windows in an indoor pool facility) isn't a good idea. Other people in the vicinity when a ball is being thrown is not a good idea. I wish I could say that I knew that *before* other people were hit with balls thrown by my children, but I must admit that experience, not predictive beliefs have led me to that conclusion. Boats are a better choice. They are harder to throw, and are therefore less risky in the hands of my sons. Since they were still learning how to play, the boats spent much of the time looking like the Titanic, as the boys tried to sink each one.

Birthday pictures were, as expected, poor. James has an upset, jealous look, and Jackson is giving his own version of a fake smile. Jackson chose pizza, but I couldn't eat much at the restaurant, because I had been recently diagnosed with celiac disease. I was fine with it, though, aside from the extraordinarily slow service that night. On a separate note, those without experience with difficult children might not understand my seemingly critical view of our service at businesses, sometimes. I do not have any ill feelings towards the workers, but if you have endured outings with difficult children, a moment or two of waiting or an unintentional mistake with an order can be devastating. I don't fault them for it, it's just one of those things that we must deal with differently than most. Anyway… when we went back to the hotel, Jackson opened his presents, giving me perfectly terrible photo opportunities. Then we ate our ice cream, and called it a day. We were to be meeting people as a part of our support group the next day. We started out the day driving to the opposite end of the city to go to the boot store. Jackson found some that he said felt good on his feet. I needed to pick up some things to bring for the support group get-together, and got some extra socks for the boys to help the boots fit better.

While we were checking out, James started acting up. He was grabbing things off of the aisle shelves, and commenting on the checker's name. Leonardo. James seemed to find this absolutely hilarious. He wouldn't stop talking and repeating his name, and referring to him as a Ninja Turtle. I was trying to catch James looking at me, to give him a "you better quit" look, but his poor eye contact aided him in avoiding me. He would not stop talking! I put our bagged purchases right on top of him, trying to get him to stop, and look at me. He just became more vocal, and pretended that I was burying him with our stuff. He was still going on about Leonardo and Ninja Turtles, and Jackson was joining right in. I couldn't get out of there fast enough. Thankfully, the guy was pleasant, and didn't seem annoyed at my children laughing at his name. I explained in the car that some people might not always be happy with their names, and making fun of them was not appropriate. Nothing came of my lecture, of course. About 3 months later, James would tell me that the checker looked like his former grandfather. That explained the anxiety and naughty behavior. Why couldn't he have just told me when we were there? He still had no trust in me, and no coping skills on his own. We were struggling with daily interactions and difficult behaviors all the time.

The support group went better than the last one had gone, as this family had hired their nanny to come in for the event. She had experience with these kind of children. She didn't, however, have experience with mine. No one was hurt, but she did mention that the boys had "a lot of energy". They resorted to watching a video well before she intended to. I, however, really made a mess of things, but the people at the support group wouldn't even know. I was eating to be polite, and had only recently begun a gluten free diet due to my celiac diagnosis. I ate some soup, thinking it was fine. I didn't really think a little bit of gluten would do much, anyway. I was fine, at first, and then wasn't feeling well. I figured that it was just because I hadn't eaten enough- any kind of social event that involves children like mine has potential for catastrophe, and I was a bit too nervous to eat much. I thought that I just needed to eat. I was feeling kind of light-headed, and not well. I rounded up the kids, thanked the hosts, and went to the car. I opened a can of pop, and started eating some almonds and gluten-free crackers I'd packed. I was thinking that eating would make me feel better. I drove a couple of miles, and decided that I needed to walk around a bit. We stopped at a store, and I told the boys that they just needed to stay with me- I was going to the bathroom, and we'd just walk for a minute before coming back to the car. Then I said- wait a minute, let me eat a few more almonds before we go in. Then James asked me "Are almonds gluten-free?" It dawned on me that gluten might be the reason for my feelings of illness- not the almonds, but something else I'd eaten. I called my mom, and sure enough, one of the first ingredients on a can of tomato soup is "wheat flour". I had consumed gluten. We were about 2 hours and 15 minutes from home, as we were on the far side of the city starting out. I didn't know if I could make it. I felt so sick, but the digestive symptoms I would have expected were not present. I had the worst headache of my life, and didn't feel like I had enough strength to even move my arms. James asked for a drink, and I didn't know if I could even unzip the cooler. I told them I was sick, but I was going to be ok. At that point, I really didn't know. He was too intent on the extremely loud video they were watching on the tablet to care, anyway. I kept making sure that I was awake, and called my poor, always helpful mother. I told her how I was feeling, and asked if I could drop the boys off at her house to watch TV for a few minutes while I tried to get better. She knew I must be really bad off, because I NEVER let the boys go anywhere without me. I didn't even walk them into the house. I watched my mom meet them at the door, and I headed home.

I hadn't lain down 2 minutes when the boys' birthmother called. I admit, I was not exactly wanting to talk right then, but my guilty feelings would not allow me to ignore her call again. I hadn't answered her call during the support group thing, and knew that she always got nervous when I didn't answer. So I answered. She talked for quite some time, and then I closed my eyes after taking a bunch of headache pills. The quiet and the medicine helped, but I was still not well. I went back to my parent's house after about an hour. I was not all the way better, but I felt like I could speak and walk again. I vowed to never eat gluten again. The boys expressed a very minimal amount of concern, but were not any less difficult during the following days when I still felt weak.

We celebrated Jackson's birthday with the rest of the family the following day. James could not handle the jealousy at all. He lost it shortly after we ate the meal, before gifts or the "dinosaur cake" I was requested to make. When we went down the cake decorating row that day for something, there was a monkey piñata. I saw that it was only $2.99, and indulged the boys. I put a bunch of these little monkeys I had bought for something else (they came in a gross), and a few other things leftover from the birthday treat bags for Jackson's class. Something happened during the piñata event that made James upset. I think he had gotten too wound up and did something he hadn't intended to- probably punching or grabbing one of the cousins. He ran off whining. At first I was upset, but within a few minutes, I realized that he was actually making really good choices. He had opted to avoid the situation (his specialty), but not cause a scene. I asked my nieces and nephew to just let him be. They did. I talked to him, telling him that he could come up and be with us for presents and dessert, but he ignored me. I told him that I was proud of him for letting Jackson have his birthday, and not ruining it. He was somewhat upset when he realized that I had wrapped a small gift for him (additional tracks for their car set) that I said he would need to wait until *his* birthday for, since he missed present-opening time. He recovered, though, despite the fact that he had somehow gotten the impression that Jackson would get to open them when James opened presents on his birthday. I don't know how he got that idea, but he was content to find out they were still going to be his, he just had to wait.

The jealousy issue didn't last too long, and the next couple of months went by without much trouble. Trouble meaning extremely difficult times, as compared with past experiences- not trouble defined in the way most people would think. I believe it was within this timeframe that I had a mini-breakdown. The day started off as "typical" as any day for us. That was the problem, actually. James had decided to cover the toilet- including the seat, handle, and top, as well as the bathroom wall, with urine. He had done it the night before, but I didn't go into the bathroom after him until nearly midnight that night. I knew it was him, because he had gone to the bathroom when I had been on the phone as they were getting ready for bed. He probably was just upset that I hadn't dedicated my entire being to him, as I was on the phone. I

192

was so angry, I almost went and woke him, so he could clean that mess up. I had even opened the door to the bedroom, but when I saw that "innocent" child sleeping, I couldn't do it.   He has a serious aversion to cleaning anything, but I was going to insist that he clean it up, even though I'd have to clean it after him anyway. It killed me to wait. I shut the bathroom door, and used the basement bathroom. I was pretty upset, and did not like the thought of that nastiness in our bathroom.

In the morning, my little bear Jackson was in his normal grumpy state. Something made him upset, but I can't remember exactly what. It could have been the cereal I served, the bowl color, the shirt I'd laid out being wrong, or just that he was grumpy. Regardless of the reason, his bowl of cereal ended up all over the floor. Thankfully he hadn't put milk on it yet. He didn't just drop the bowl once, he saw to it that it was flung with such effort that fruit loops would be spread all over the house, from one wall to the other. I said that he must not be hungry, and he could just eat at daycare instead. Then he started walking on the cereal. I don't know how I didn't blow my top right then. I really don't. We didn't have time in the morning before school and work to get the house cleaned up. I closed the door, and walked out of the house trying to be hopeful that the evening would not be completely taken up with fits over the clean-up. I closed my eyes and shook my head at the thought of the mess in our home as the boys buckled up. I dropped them off at the building where they are to be, ready to begin the work day. As I drove down the street to the building where I work, it suddenly hit me that I had perceived this day as fine. Maybe not great, but fine. What had happened to me? When did it become normal for me to leave a bathroom covered in urine, and fruit loops all over the house? I cried. I felt so deflated. I couldn't believe that in my mind, that particular morning was typical. When I seemed to grasp that this way of life, this new normal, was *our* life, I didn't know what to think. I knew the boys were getting better. I knew things were going to be fine, eventually. Every day was hard, though, without a doubt. Even though I knew in my heart that our family was in the process of healing, times were tough. I came to terms with the fact that even though fruit loops and urine all over the house wasn't rock bottom (we'd already been there), there was still only one way to go. Things were going to get better. They surely couldn't get much worse.

Finally Mom

The process in which my name was changed to "Mama" by Jackson was just around the time of his 5th birthday, and the transition to consistent use came pretty quickly. He had begun to kind of play around with the term, in a sing-song sort of manner. Then he would do this baby act, and call me Mama. It was over a very short period of time, and I had become Mama. It was nice. James still wouldn't go along with it, but stopped "correcting" Jackson by rephrasing what he had said to eliminate the term. Before too long, James would refer to me using "Mama" when talking with Jackson, but it would quite a while after that before he would use the name to address me. Regardless, it felt good. I knew that this was a big step for them. They were now beginning to think of me as their mother.

As things were beginning to get better, I had to deal with my own ups and downs due to excessive optimism. I kept seeing the bright future, only to be brought back down to reality with what was in front of me. I wanted my children to be "normal", but knew that our definition of normal was just not the same as everyone else's. I made sure I kept up with every effort to support attachment, and tried give my kids the experiences in life that they deserve. I would put a note in James's lunchbox every day, and had since he'd been with me. I would write "I love you", or "Good Luck with spelling." He told me "I don't ever really read your notes." I was hurt, but didn't give up. He was on a trivia kick with my dad, so I would write a trivia question in his snack bag, and put the answer in his lunch box. No luck. He still would not read my notes. I wish I could say that the trivia plan worked, but maybe next year. He only read my notes maybe 3 times in all. Once was right after I had been upset with him for eating *only* his cookies I'd put in his lunch, with the note saying "I love you! Eat your sandwich and fruit FIRST!"

Another experience involving a huge let-down was one that I thought was really great at first. My mom had decided to get tickets for all of the grandkids to go to see this magic show that was being performed at our local theater. Honestly, I had been hesitant to agree to go in the first place. It was really late for a school night, and these kind of things never turned out well for us. I planned carefully to prepare things to minimize problems. Upon arriving at the show, I seated the boys on either side of me, with my mom on Jackson's other side, and my sister next to James. I politely requested that the cousins not mess with the boys. They did well- all of them. The boys seemed to really enjoy the magic show. James, who would never "connect" with me visually, kept looking at me with his excitement and awe during the show. It was amazing. He was sharing his excitement *with* me. That had never happened before. There was only one time that James got upset. A trick scared him, and he worried that someone was going to be cut. He turned away, into his seat, but towards me. He sought me out for comfort, sort of. We all left talking about the show, and we went home, without any fits. They took baths and got into bed, still content and sharing about the show. Jackson couldn't take a bath and get in bed without a fit on a *normal* night. I was ecstatic! I called my mom to tell her how much it meant to me that she had taken us to the show. It was the first time we'd planned to do something (I let them know only just before we went), actually gone, and left happy, with no fits in between.

The only negative part was James becoming scared during the one trick, but that was almost a guarantee with whatever we might be watching. He recovered well, which is an accomplishment in and of itself. I was almost in tears because I was so pleased about the way the evening had gone. They talked about it the next day. It was so nice. The event was on Tuesday. I had shared with the therapist in an email about the wonderful event we'd experienced, and my elation regarding the positive outcome. At therapy on Friday, as always, she asked James about the best part of the week. This topic always bothered me, because no matter what we had done, James never recalled it. I suppose that it is just hard for these kids to hold on to anything positive. It was still hard for me to witness, every week. This week was going to be different. I just *knew* that this time he'd remember. He was going to tell about the show. The therapist guided him. I tried to give some direction, too. She said "You didn't get to do anything special this week?" He said "No". I said "We did something different... on Tuesday. Remember?" He was stumped. He thought and then his face lit up. My excitement was beginning to grow. He said, "Oh, yeah! I forgot my backpack and had to eat school lunch!" I was really disappointed. I became more so when I asked "Was that really the best part of Tuesday? You hate to eat school lunch. You didn't even like it! I know that *I* was upset because you didn't really eat a healthy meal for lunch, and then we had fast food that night." Still nothing from him, even though "fast food" should have been a clue. We only eat fast food before evening events or after therapy- never just on a weeknight without reason. He finally said, with wide, knowing eyes, "I remember now! I only ate the broccoli from the school lunch and I had broccoli burps all day." This was the day he broke the table at therapy. When he found out what he had forgotten, he was actually upset. I guess that's a good thing, since he was beginning to realize that the event might have been a memory worth holding on to. He couldn't recall the memory on his own, though, which saddened me. We had talked so much about it, and we'd had a lot of fun. I thought it was great that we had really gotten through something enjoyable, and back home for baths and bed without fits. It was a great accomplishment. I just couldn't believe that he could remember the insignificant details of that particular day, but not the one event I thought was memorable. This was the start of a bit of a rough phase for James.

With the spring, came memories of past encounters with "Nana". James was worried everywhere he went. He'd had only one problem at school (which they chose not to inform me about) involving him biting another child. The other child had tickled James on his leg, which happens to be a sensitive and triggering location for him. He bit the kid. James did not tell me about this, but because I work with children from his class, I heard the story. I really would have thought that someone from the school would have let me know, however, since he had been sent to the behavior office, and had many bite marks all over his arm from biting himself. Anyway, I guess they wanted to keep me in the dark so I would still be the only one that ever saw him act inappropriately. Second graders don't typically bite one another, and their decision to keep pretending didn't change the fact that he did have problems.

The fear of "Nana" caused James enormous stress. He was worried about the upcoming field trips, which gave me another opportunity at conferences to be the "crazy mom". There were several end of the year activities that were alarming to him, and I was concerned about him watching videos as the school year came to a close. That's common, I know, and he did not do well with movies. Curious George, Kung Fu Panda, Paddington, you name it, he was scared of it. He had begun biting himself

198

constantly, which I warned the teacher of. I asked if he could just go read a book in the hall or something if he showed signs of being agitated. I specifically described the behaviors to watch for: biting himself, running out of the room, ducking his head, turning around, climbing on furniture, kicking his feet, standing on his head, etc. I had talked with James about this issue, and he said that he actually *wanted* me to address it with his teacher. Even though he wanted me to speak with her, his anxiety was very high. While I talked during the parent/teacher conference, he chose to toss a stuffed toy at the ceiling repeatedly, despite my pleas to stop. The response from the teacher was, of course, "It's ok." She seemed responsive to my requests to monitor him during movies, but she must not have completely grasped what I was trying to tell her. He still came home with self-inflicted bite marks on his arm from watching movies that had any possible risk for someone to be hurt, and any movies that had shadows, and any movies that had affection between characters depicted. Even animated turtle affection. Yes, his fears were irrational, but they were real. The teacher never did get that, or at least she didn't admit it.

I would find out about a month later, while working with kids from his class, that he must have had some kind of display of problems, however. While I was showing a movie to a group of children on a rainy day during the first week of summer, one child said, from across the room to James, "It's ok, James, the dog's going to be ok, he won't get hurt." Only someone who had witnessed James having a reaction to such a scene would have known. I was watching James for reaction the whole time, and although he was displaying signs of anxiety, he hadn't done anything that would have been obvious to most people. He had put his head down, and sucked on his arm, but not made any sounds. I was actually showing the movie almost as a test- I wanted to see if he acted that way while part of a group of children. My sister seemed to think that he acted scared just for my benefit. Although I was in the room, I made sure that I was not in sight of him during the movie. He still showed anxiety at the slightest hint of affection or violence. I'm still curious about what happened at school, but I guess I'll never know. If they got a taste of what I see every day, they decided to keep it to themselves.

School field trips and activities were practically every day events during the last few weeks of school. That spring was difficult for James. He was edgy and whiny. He was really mean to Jackson, too. He was becoming agitated at everything, just as Jackson had done in the past. I couldn't say anything that would please him. He would just come up with a negative statement. He had gotten upset at therapy (the day of the magic show incident), and tried to climb under a small table. The leg had been broken, and our therapist said that he needed to do a job to earn a dollar from me to get some super glue to fix the table. James had never actually completed any task I requested of him. I was under the false notion that because the therapist had suggested it, it would be so. It was not the case. He couldn't pick up his clothes, put dishes in the sink (actually, once he had tried, but when the glass in the sink was shattered as he threw his cereal bowl in, I requested the dishes to be placed *beside* the sink, but it didn't happen). I had asked him to clean up the sand from his shoes, to put his shoes in the basket, and a bunch of other tasks well within his ability to perform. He just couldn't do any of them. Rewards and consequences had no impact on his decision to avoid compliance. To earn the money for the super glue, I thought very carefully about what to ask him to do. I didn't want it to be something he had to do for several days, as the risk of failure was high. I wanted something that he had to put a bit of effort into, but not something too challenging. I wanted him to feel good about completing the task, and make sure that it really wasn't beyond his ability so frustration wouldn't prevent him from finishing. I finally came up with what I thought was a good job for him. The task I asked of him was to pick up the leaves that had blown against our fence and put them into bags. We (I) had raked during the fall, but this house has great big trees, and in a pile right up against the fence, there were leaves, just waiting to be picked up and put into bags. I had demonstrated what to do, and gotten some of it done, but passed it off to James, as a way for him to complete the task to earn the dollar to fix the table. He refused. The dying cow returned. The whole town knew about it. It was a great show. It was, of course, "too hard" for a nearly 8 year old boy to pick leaves up and place them in a bag. Anyone in the surrounding area must have been thinking that I was asking that "poor child" to dig a swimming pool with a spoon. His noteworthy performance didn't end with declaring the "work" too hard. Any time I tried to walk towards him, to try and talk with him, he covered his body, then ran in panic, as if I were a murderer. Anyone with a view would have seen a terrified child and an angry mother. Their perceptions, while somewhat accurate, would not even begin to describe the whole story.

Anyway, we went back to therapy that week without him completing the task. This happened for 2 weeks. The therapist then said that he would need to pay her with something of his until he completed his job. I was initially on board. It sounded like a great idea. When he blew it, as I should have expected, by choosing not to do his job, I was upset. I now had to be the one to find something that would be significant to him to have the therapist hang on to. I thought and thought about what to bring. I was so stressed. He didn't really care about anything. I could bring his tablet, but that was nothing new for him to lose. He would just look over Jackson's shoulder and be content. He had just gotten these new little battery-operated toys for Easter that he had practically begged for. He had memories of them from his former grandmother's house, he said. I got them, but he had only played with them once, for less than a minute. The only thing I could think of that would get his attention was his bike, the one thing (after he finally learned to ride it) that he admitted enjoying. I called my mom. I went over my options. She was just as puzzled. We finally agreed that although the bike was big, there was really nothing else. The only close second was his stuffed shark that he finally had seemed to develop a preference for as far as something to sleep with.

I didn't remind him about the plan. I didn't want to deal with the all-night fit. He knew the agreement, yet chose to avoid his task for retribution. After the boys were asleep, I remember walking to the garage in an odd state of emotion. My head was spinning. For me, it was similar to the feeling you get when you hear some *really* bad news, and are trying to process it. Any clarity of thinking was gone. I did what I had to do, but my mind was a million miles away. This was hard. I didn't want to bring the bike. I didn't want to do that to my son. I knew that the therapist wouldn't really keep his bike, but my thoughts were in a whirlwind. What if James never decided to get those stupid leaves picked up? What if he compares me to "Nana", throwing his toys away with no regard for his feelings? Is this really necessary? Why wouldn't he just pick up those leaves? Why didn't I just give him another job? What if he goes into a deep depression because of this? I finally escaped those thoughts, only to have the two hour drive the next day to go over them again. I became more and more nervous the closer we got to the therapist's office. I had called my mom and tried to calm myself, seeking reassurance that this was what I had to do. I didn't bring the bike in when we arrived. My session was first, and I must have been a wreck. I think the therapist took pity on me, and gave him a different option for my benefit. He was still going to have to do the leaves, but he was not going to be able to participate in any of the fun things going on at school during the last few weeks, if he did not do his job. I left therapy that day with a great sense of relief. I told James how lucky he was that our therapist was so kind. He didn't believe me about the bike until he saw it in our trunk when we got home. We went to therapy on Fridays, so he had until Wednesday before the first school-related activity was to occur. It was not a full-class event, just a couple of kids from his class and the other second grade class with the teachers at a restaurant. It was a social kind of thing. He seemed happy about the idea of going.

Meanwhile, Jackson had been incredibly helpful, and I'd found all sorts of little jobs for him to do that James refused to help with. Then came the egg-cracking for pancakes, and when I only asked Jackson, James became jealous enough to want to help. I said that if he wanted to do jobs, I would ask him only after he had picked up the leaves, since I'd asked him to do that job first. Jackson was really taking the "job" thing to heart, and was being extremely helpful. Even though I wasn't asking James to do any type of extra job, I had asked both of them to clean the trash from Friday out of the car, which is a routine request. There are always wrappers, empty juice box containers and snack baggies left from our long car ride. James rarely brings in anything from the car, so his side is typically a mess. James, as usual, refused to help. Jackson saw to it to make that car cleaner than usual. I had told him that he could leave the side that James sits on for him to take care of, but he lifted the booster and retrieved more junk than I realized could be compiled in only a week's time. I was proud. I decided that Jackson deserved a reward. When I told him so, he beamed. James just increased his volume of moaning sounds. When I said that I would put a new game on his tablet, Jackson was overjoyed, but James had the opposite reaction. He told me how unfair it was, but I ignored his pleas. I simply reminded him that the leaves were still outside. He was furious. I think he broke several plastic bags while kicking and tearing them apart outside. I watched through the window. He then took the shovel that I had forbidden him to use because he had tried to use it inappropriately (swinging at his brother) and whacked at the clothesline. We hadn't used the clothesline except to hang up carpet squares when the basement had flooded, but it was broken, nonetheless. I have to give him some credit, though. After looking at what he had done, and realizing that he couldn't reach the bar to put the line back through even if it wasn't snapped, he trudged back to the house. He came to me and told me what had happened. I told him that I was very proud of him for telling the truth. I asked what happened, and he told me that he was mad, took the shovel and hit the clothesline. I praised him again for telling the truth. I said that we'd figure out how to deal with that later, and reminded him that the leaves were still there. He saw Jackson playing his new game, and could not tear himself away from watching him play. I actually got a little irritated that he enjoyed watching him play it so much. I wondered why he didn't just get those leaves put away and see if he could earn the game like Jackson.

The next day he must have reached that conclusion himself. It might have been because I made brownies requiring eggs again, too. He was really wanting to crack some eggs. He asked about the game, and what he'd have to do to get it. I said that he'd have to be helpful for a while, and he'd have to start by doing his job. I added that he didn't really have to go to the Wednesday night thing even if he did do his job. I also stated that he'd have to do an extra job to pay for a new line for the clothesline, but it wouldn't be that day. He obviously didn't *really* want to hear my response, because he had a good little fit. He quieted down and edged himself over to get a view of Jackson playing his new game. After I caught Jackson letting James have a turn, I said that the game was only for hard workers. Jackson could not let James play the game. James needed to earn it. Much to my surprise, James didn't fall on the floor into a fit. He grabbed another bag and went out to do the leaves. He didn't do the greatest job, but he worked hard for all of about 20 minutes. It would have been faster, but I had him pick up the pieces of the bags he'd torn apart, too. Upon finishing, he was bursting with pride. The first thing he said after he finished was "I don't really want to go on Wednesday". The difficulty with the job had not initially been tied to the school event, but when it became a part of it, he decided to use it. He could choose not to do the job, and avoid the school event. It was brilliant. No one would have been the wiser had it not been for that enticing video game. I let the teacher know about the problem. I had talked with James and concluded that he was worried about one of his former family members being there. Local establishments were (and are) sources of anxiety for him, even if "Nana" never actually went there with him. Despite reassurance that the likelihood of someone from his first family being there was minimal, and even with my offer to stay at the restaurant, he declined. I made the reasons clear to the teacher, and thought that the problem was taken care of. I was wrong. I can't fault the teacher's intentions. I hope, with great worry, that my sincere dedication to the students I work with has not led me to do anything harmful to kids like mine. James was fortunate to have such a caring teacher, but she did not understand the unique problems that he has. She tried to convince him to come. She called me, and told me how she reassured him that he would be safe, and said she asked him "Haven't I kept you safe?" My poor son, who had finally opened up to me about his real fears, was unintentionally being bullied into changing his mind about going. The chosen few children that week were apparently not randomly chosen. One child, with whom the teacher had social connections to, had not been able to have people over for his birthday, and it had been arranged for his buddies to have their turns at the same time, so they could have a mini celebration. My son's difficulties were making this a problem for the plan. I did find it odd that these children considered my son a good friend. James hadn't spoken much of either of the boys he was to meet with. I was glad that his behavior hadn't caused him to be rejected as I had thought it had. I sent a note with James saying that I would be very open to getting together with the family, but that the plans for the evening wouldn't work out for us. I invited them to meet with us, and left our number, but no one ever called.

James was a mess. He was finally starting to have real feelings, and was having some guilt about not going. I was honest, and told him that other people didn't understand what it was like for him. Their hearts were healthy. One day, his would be, too. In the meantime, we just have to go on and do what we have to until he can have fun participating in those kind of things. I was upset that the teacher had tried to convince him to go. I was also worried that I might have done the same thing before truly understanding what traumatized children endure. I chose not to address the issue with her. There were only a few weeks left of school. That was enough time for me to seal the deal on winning the crazy mom contest, even without another formal discussion. There were several school trips planned. One was to the nursing home, which triggers his trauma because any really old lady with a wrinkled, pockmarked, or dry complexion he felt looked like "Nana". I let him skip it, and picked him up before they left. The next one was to the brown bag concert. The same one that the former grandmother had invaded. He was absolutely opposed even if I went with his class. One was to the police station, which he declined (he recalled going there before his birthmother went away, and visiting someone with "Papa"). The other trip was to the library and museum. He had actually wanted to go on that one at first, until I guessed that they would likely eat in the same park where the brown bag concerts are held. I asked if he still wanted to go if that was where they were eating, and he said no. I told him that I would call the teacher to find out, and if they were going to eat there, I would just come pick him up after the first part of the trip. He said that's what he wanted me to do. I called to find out the lunch plans, and the teacher acted like I was nuts. It was a rainy day, so they ended up eating somewhere in the museum. He survived one trip without much trouble.

Another was to the same zoo that I had taken them to with "Nana" right after getting them. I didn't realize that he would have any problems going there, at first. It was actually the last field trip he was to go on. It was planned for very last week of school, and it happened to fall on my birthday. When the information came home, we were talking about the events coming up, and he said that he would rather just spend time with me since it was my birthday. I initially fell for it, thinking the glorious day had finally come... my son wanted to be with me! The joy lasted less than an hour, until I came down from the clouds and faced reality. There was no way he really wanted to be with me. What was the ploy? Did he want me to feel like he was sacrificing something for me? Did he feel like he was supposed to do that? I didn't say too much, but the very next day he went to school telling everyone (it's nice to have "ears" around) that he wasn't going to go on the field trip because his mom wanted him to be with her on her birthday.

I had a little talk with him. I was beginning to suspect that the zoo was the problem, but wanted him to tell me himself. I said that it made me sound very selfish to make my little boy miss his field trip just to be with me on my birthday. I asked what the real reason was. First, he said "I won't get to see anything, there will be too many people." I reminded him that we take lots more kids during our summer field trips. Then he said "If I can't feed the animals, I don't even want to go." I inquired further, because I figured he wanted to would blame me for not sending money to feed the animals, because I opt not to send spending money on field trips. Nope, he just didn't think he'd get to feed the animals. Then I asked "What if it was to the same place that your first field trip was- the science museum?" He said that he'd go again to that one. Then I was getting a little bold. I asked if he was *worried* about going to that zoo. He said "yes". I felt relief. "That's it," I thought. Then I pressed on, asking what it was about the zoo that worried him. He started talking, and I'm sure my heart skipped a beat. I was hearing the words that I had prepared myself for... "I keep thinking that someone might be there," he said. I asked "Who do you think might be there that would worry you?" I was full of confidence that he would soon reveal his fear that "Nana" might be there since we had gone there with her before. He took a deep breath, ready to share, ready to open up. I held my breath, waiting for him to show his trust in me by sharing this enormous fear. He started to talk, and said "my basketball coach from last year." The tension was broken. I was confused. Where on earth had that come from? His basketball coach? He had played for a different school team. The coach was a parent of a child on the team. From the other school. Who we never see. It took me a moment to figure out what had just happened. I had prepared myself for him to open up and share that the memories of "Nana" at that zoo were upsetting him. I had to come up with a different approach to that response. I asked him why that upset him. I never noticed him being apprehensive around that guy, but he was constantly in his galloping fairy mode then, so it would have been hard to tell. He said that the coach always carried a knife. He did- it was a pocket knife. Many men around here carry pocket knives. I asked why he thought that the coach might be there, and James couldn't tell me. I kind of fed him the next question, letting him know that I thought he might be worried about "Nana". He acted (not very well, either) as if he had never thought of that, but admitted that he probably felt that way. We dropped it, and he was not to go on that trip.

As for the brown bag concert, I soon realized that I couldn't go even if he would have been better if I were to attend. Somehow, the field trip for my preschool class had fallen on the same day again, even though the year prior both events had been a week later- and James had attended a different school. I was in a dilemma. I was taking my class to the *same* zoo that we had gone to with the former grandmother. James had already said that he didn't want to go there with his class for the next field trip, and now, he would have to come with me anyway. I didn't give him an option, because there wasn't really one to give. He told me, though, that he would rather go to the zoo with me than go to that park again. So we went. The therapist had suggested I give him a task to keep him occupied and avoid the behaviors and anxiety associated with trauma triggers. It worked really well except during lunch. I had decided to bring Jackson along, too. It was actually a group of children his age anyway, and I wouldn't get back in time to pick him up for the afternoon as I usually did. So, together, they made a scene at lunch, and a few other minor issues emerged but nothing too serious. Jackson was a bit of a handful, but it wasn't a terrible show he put on. He was acting a little weird, but it wasn't anything that drew a considerable amount of attention. He was just doing little things that I asked him not to- crawling under the benches, for example. I was glad when it was all over, but I didn't realize how much the experience had actually effected the boys, especially Jackson, until later. When we went to therapy, we talked about the trip, and Jackson expressed that he wasn't happy on the trip. I thought he might have been jealous, since there were so many other children that I needed to attend to. I thought he might have been feeling a little nervous with the other kids and some of the parents. He said he was "scared". The therapist and I were working to help him describe what made him feel that way.

After many "wrong" suggestions, I finally asked if he felt that way because we had been to that zoo before. He said yes. I was floored. I knew that James was worried about the zoo, but I didn't realize that Jackson had the same feelings. When we had gone to that zoo with "Nana", Jackson was barely 3 years old. He'd only been with me for a couple of weeks at that time. He couldn't recall much of anything that we had done for the whole first year together, but that particular zoo caused him anxiety and fear. His odd behaviors that I thought were more of a "show-off" kind of thing, were instead related to the memories that the location had triggered. I knew that the "Nana" relationship was not a good one, but when I came to know that Jackson had such strong feelings about a place he associated with her, almost 2 years later, I realized that whatever that woman did (or didn't do) to them was very significant. I just can't imagine how she must have made them feel.

Another day that James missed was because we had to get Jackson's teeth taken care of. Jackson had a filling in his tooth come out, and I brought him back to the dentist. He'd had several fillings put in the last time we'd gone to the dentist. The dentist gave him the laughing gas again, but before he'd even touched him, Jackson started screaming. The dentist said that we'd need a specialist, as he hadn't even touched Jackson yet and he'd reacted so severely. I think that when he had the fillings put in, there must have been a time when they'd touched a nerve. He'd done really well until the end that time, but now wouldn't let anyone close. We had to arrange for sedation. There was no place local that would do it, so I set it up near the city where we go to therapy, because the only other option was 2 ½ hours in a different direction. I got it set so we could get the dental work done, and still go to therapy afterwards. I kept James out of school the whole day instead of leaving at noon, and even had to cancel my preschool class so my mom could come. The anesthesiologist suggested having another driver, I needed someone to keep James, and there really wasn't anyone else available. I might have risked having James keep occupied with his tablet, but his behavior during our first visit to that dentist weighed heavily on my decision to have another adult with him. I had scheduled James to have an orthodontic evaluation done on the same day as Jackson's initial appointment. The office called and told me that they changed my appointment time to be 30 minutes later. I said that was fine, and didn't think anything of it.

The day of the appointment, I was very close to arriving at their office when they called to say that I was late for our appointment. Apparently they didn't change both appointments, which were staggered- only one. When we arrived, they immediately took us back and began to examine James to orthodontic needs. I had come across orthodontic information by accident, and then realized that maybe, just maybe, some of James's horrible eating habits might *not* be RAD related. I began to feel really guilty. I still think that his overstuffing, side biting, and open mouth chewing is somewhat related to the RAD issues, because it has improved somewhat and the braces don't go on until next month. I was really upset with myself for a while, thinking that I had been getting after him so much about these disgusting eating habits, only to find out that his teeth might have contributed to the problem. I finally realized that although part of it could be due to his teeth, he couldn't blame all of his issues on that. His teeth did *not* cause him to eat with his fingers, use the silverware to scratch the table, tap his utensils constantly, stuff his mouth until it wouldn't close, or use a spoon for meat and a fork for soup, just to irritate me. I released some of my guilt when I realized that orthodontics weren't going to fix *all* of the problems.

211

Regardless, while James was being looked at, they came to get Jackson. I went with him, but was very worried leaving James, even though they were taking x-rays and appeared that they'd be busy with him for a while. While with Jackson, the dentist discovered that he had new cavities. Big ones. He would need several crowns, in addition to replacing the filling. I couldn't figure out what had happened. He had a few cavities last check-up, but it was not that long ago. The other dentist hadn't mentioned anything when I'd brought him in to have the filling replaced. I would find out one evening what had probably been occurring for months. My mom got us a candy dispenser. I used it for little treats for the boys. One warm evening, as winter was coming to an end, I put Jackson in a lightweight pair of athletic pants and shirt to sleep in. He really likes blanket sleepers, but it was too warm that evening, and I hadn't yet retrieved the box of spring clothing with the cooler pajamas in it. He had his hand on his pocket (which his other pajamas didn't have), and I asked what he had. That's when I realized that he had something in his mouth. I saw the candy. He had been getting candy after brushing his teeth, probably every night, as I went to put the laundry from the bathroom into the laundry room. That explained the tooth damage.

Anyway, at the dentist while Jackson and I were in a little room, and James was not in sight, I heard a loud crash. I knew it was James. I felt guilty thinking that, though. I thought that I must be the most negative person ever. Why would I think that my son had made that crash? After explaining the unique needs of Jackson to the dentist, since Jackson had not exactly been cooperative (demonstrating the reason he required sedation), we finally were led back to where James was. There he was, with 2 staff members, doing the one thing he knew he shouldn't be doing. I hadn't thought to tell him no, but he would have done it anyway. I guess that his former grandfather had asked for rubber gloves to blow up to make balloon/balls/chickens out of when they went to the doctor. James asked me all the time to make the doctors give some to us. I explained that I had boxes and boxes of rubber gloves at work, and if he wanted any, he could have some from there. He never asked. So, here they were, the dental assistants cleaning up a large tray of items, and James running around, bouncing the stupid chicken-glove-balls all over, and crashing into everything. I am surprised they even allowed us to continue to be seen in their office. I was seriously displeased. I was even more displeased as the dentist shared with me the procedures necessary for orthodontics, and the cost. What was most upsetting was the fact that my sons were bouncing all over. James was crawling over the row of chairs in the room, Jackson underneath with his new toy car he'd gotten from the dentist.

I was ready to get out of there, but there was another stop on the way out. This was the least pleasant. The finance lady was not a fan of children (or at least *my* children). The boys were not behaving very well, anyway. There were things to touch, and they had those horrible chicken-glove-balls, and now 2 toy cars. There were chairs to make the cars ramp off of, and crawl over and through. The lady went on talking to me, acting as if the chaos alongside her wasn't really there. I left there not wanting to ever go back.

When we did return for Jackson to get his dental work done, things were slightly better. James had earned that game he wanted, so his tablet kept him busy. My mom kept him in the car for a good share of the time, which was better than kicking the other kids off of the video game system the dentist's waiting room had. The biggest complication was that Jackson did not want to wake up in a timely manner. He took way longer than expected, and was extremely groggy. He couldn't walk. He was a little funny, I'll admit, but I sincerely hope that we don't have to go through it again. He, upon waking and seeing his arm with a bandage on it, slurring his speech, looked up at the anesthesiologist with disgust, and said "You gave me a shot".

We headed to therapy, very late. I knew he wouldn't be able to participate much, but at least James wouldn't miss his session. Jackson wanted to play games on his tablet on the way to therapy. His new favorite was a racing game. For him, it must have been like one of those drunk driving simulators. He said there were two cars, and he kept crashing. Jackson has no tolerance for frustration, so not being able to play well really upset him, even in his inebriated state. His determination wasn't effected by the medication, however, so he'd try, crash, and scream. Try, crash, and scream. He doesn't remember any of it.

He had to have one of the caps polished down the following week, because his bite wasn't the way it needed to be. The dentist assured me that he couldn't feel a thing, but you wouldn't know it the way he reacted. There was one good thing that came from it, though. He retreated to me for comfort. He held my hand and reached for me. There was a time when I couldn't approach him, and now, my son felt safe in my arms. It was a good feeling. Good enough to give me the strength to walk out of the dentist's office with my head held high. They'd shut the doors to the little room where Jackson was being worked on to muffle his screams. When we walked out, I heard some of the dental staff say "Was that the screamer?" I am pretty sure it wasn't my imagination that we got more stares than usual as we exited the office. I didn't care. My sweaty little boy was clutching me. He held me tightly, but he was not in a panicked state. He felt safe. His tears had stopped when he got into my arms. He now accepted me to be the one to provide the comfort that he needed. That was an amazing feeling.

James was missing a lot of school during the last part of the year, and the dentist day was the only non-PTSD related absence. He also missed the second grade sleepover, which was on a therapy night anyway, and he missed field day. I was worried about field day, because he doesn't handle not being the best at anything. He was worried because it wasn't all inside the fence at school. There were some things held in the adjacent park (another place we'd met "Nana"). I could not attend the field day events, as it was my preschool graduation day. I had to be there. I offered my dad (who was willing) to watch for a while, but he couldn't stay all morning. James wanted someone with him for the whole time. I said we couldn't do that, but he could stay with me. We had therapy that day, too. I had just scheduled it an hour later so I could get the preschool stuff done. James stayed with me, and that was that. The child never had a sick day at school, but missed every Friday afternoon for therapy, and almost the whole month of May. The school counted each of those field trip and event days that he missed as "unexcused" absences. The day I kept him out because I had to bring Jackson to the dentist was counted as "excused", but the days he had to miss to keep him emotionally stable were not. Even though it really doesn't matter, I was a little upset. My son had an excuse. The police station day, he'd considered going for a while. He'd made himself sick with worry, and I finally just said that I was going to call the school in the morning and say he wasn't feeling well. That was the truth. He wasn't feeling well, and he was making himself sick worrying about it. I am fairly confident that if I had allowed him to stew much longer over the possibility of going, he would have ended up throwing up. To me, that meant he was "sick"- even if he didn't have a virus. He had honestly never missed school for being sick, but the reason I gave to the office implied that he *was* ill. That day, too, was counted as "unexcused". It could be that they saw him later in the day because he had to accompany me to kindergarten round up with Jackson, who knows? I guess those who determine which excuses are valid have never parented a child with PTSD.

215

Tough Times Aren't so Tough Anymore

James started changing at about this time. Something happened right before his 8th birthday. We were just shy of 2 years together. He finally broke through, and decided to get better. Things became easier all around. Jackson was having some minor problems, mostly with adjusting to the new routine, since he couldn't spend afternoons with me anymore, but with James acting better, everything was easier. My sons played together, finally. It took almost 2 years for them to be able to play together. They couldn't even play *near* each other before. Jackson had tried, but James wouldn't allow it. He would cheat, deliberately destroy, or just rudely exclude Jackson. He was impossible. We tried playing games, but it didn't work. The first time we successfully played a game together I couldn't believe it. I was scared to play again. I was thrilled that we'd made it through a game. There was a winner and a loser, and we still had all the pieces in front of us. I had a strange feeling that something was missing. I realized that it was the screaming, pouting, and destruction. All I saw was contentedness. James asked if we could play again, and I didn't know what to say. I prayed that he would win, since Jackson had won the first time. It would make the day end well. I wanted it so badly. Somehow, I won the next game, and there was no way to make it so I could change what I

216

had been dealt. I cringed as I laid my card down. I was scared to look up to see the boys' faces. When I did, I was shocked to see that they were fine. We played again, and James finally won. Jackson had ducked out by this time, but I was still feeling on top of the world. We had played a game together.

Playing together was such a welcome new concept. I had waited so long to witness them playing like "normal" children. I had dreamt of the possibilities of a clean house and attempting hobbies as I had in the past. I found myself watching and enjoying the boys as they played instead of ever actually getting to those tasks. It was so nice.

Once, while visiting my cousin's house on Memorial Day, I was enjoying watching the boys play. Playing in the yard for more than a few minutes was unheard of. Some kind of disastrous event had always forced the "play" to end. Watching them play made me so happy. I was still nervous, but excited and overly optimistic about the future. As they were playing ball in my cousin's yard, the first real accidental injury between the boys occurred. Accidents didn't happen, because intentional injuries had always resulted in the activity being stopped. They crashed into each other, and both fell to the ground. James has a tendency to have an exaggerated reaction to any possibility of injury, so his wails didn't alarm me too much. Jackson was not crying, but was holding his head. I was walking slowly towards them, trying not to escalate the situation or intensify any anxiety. Jackson was closest, so I picked him up and went to James. I looked them over. Jackson was bleeding, and finally starting to cry a little. James had stopped howling and was appearing to put on a brave face. I asked my cousin for some paper towels, and tried to figure out what had happened. James was holding his face. I asked what hurt, and he said his teeth. They were a bit loose, but not close to falling out. I was remembering that the orthodontist had said that the risk of knocking his teeth out was high, and felt relieved that his teeth were still in his mouth.

Jackson had two "teeth marks" in the top of his head. It wasn't an injury that required an emergency room visit, but significant nonetheless. He allowed me to clean him up, but refused ice. While I was tending to his wound, James was hanging around. He looked upset. I asked him "Are you OK? Do you hurt anywhere else?" He shook his head "no", but then said words that had never spontaneously been spoken by him before. He said "I'm sorry. I didn't mean to hurt Jackson. That's gotta hurt." James hung his head in shame. I can't describe the feeling I had right then. I was a bit overwhelmed. There had been so many intense emotions over such a short period of time. I had been so pleased to see them playing together, worried over the injuries, relieved when they were not seriously wounded, and finally shocked at hearing those words from James. He was apologetic, and had expressed empathy. Had I heard correctly? I had to think through what had just happened. James had shown remorse and empathy. It was so unexpected. I feel so guilty about having such positive thoughts right then, as my children were both physically injured, but this was significant progress. James had not displayed empathy in that way, and showing compassion for his brother was certainly remarkable.

I explained to James that it really wasn't his fault. It was an accident. They were both playing together, and ran into each other. I reminded him that he was actually hurt, too. It wasn't just Jackson that was hurt. I was impressed with both of them. I think they enjoyed having their injuries tended to a bit too much, but I indulged. They both took ibuprofen for a couple days, but then seemed fine. There are two little scars on Jackson's head that are only slightly visible after a haircut, but the memory of the boys' interactions that day was the real lasting impression. James and Jackson were forming a real relationship.

The video games, while I despised them at first, actually seemed to be bringing the boys closer together. James lacks the motor skills (since he still has trouble relaxing and controlling his body) to be successful at some things, and Jackson is younger and sometimes less capable in other ways. They started talking about their games, and giving each other tips. Everything was coming together, even when the games were turned off. The drive to work became pleasant. Mealtime transformed from a constant battle to an agreeable experience. It happened almost overnight. Even my parents, including my dad, noticed. Once, after a conversation we all had about a bunch of the school-age kids not knowing our own state capital, my dad began giving James state capital trivia. This was several months before the transformation happened. The trivia game often had resulted in one or both boys leaving the table. Jackson, the little smarty-pants, caught on, and was soon able to name nearly as many capitals as James. James would become really upset and become discouraged if Jackson got one first. He wouldn't let Jackson say the ones that my dad specifically gave to him. Then Jackson would run off crying. The game was not fun, but the boys demanded it of my dad all the time. One day, we all noticed it. They had taken turns. No one left the table upset. They had given each other hints for the correct answers. It was almost like they were different children. Changes were actually noticeable. Little accomplishments became daily events. We were able to get out of the house in the morning without fits. James would allow Jackson to have a turn at things. Jackson started to make his own choices. James became helpful, and he began to claim me as his mother. He had played with the term for me for a while, and I had to declare, without any doubt, that he was not to call me by the name "second mother" as he attempted to. I did not feel as if that was a very endearing name. He went back and forth, but, as Jackson did, seems to have settled on "Mama", which is what I call my mom, too. It works for me. It is a whole new life, now. We are nowhere near healed, I know. They remind me daily, as does the excitement I feel for the tiniest accomplishments. Just the other day, I heard them laugh together- really laugh- for the first time. They had laughed, sort of, before, but not like this. Usually there was someone being teased or hurt when they laughed before. They laughed together while playing. They enjoyed each other. My sons, while biologically related from the start, are finally brothers. It's a new concept.

My reminders of the boys' difficulties are not always obvious to everyone, but they are constantly present. Now, at least, I have the understanding, and sometimes the sense of humor necessary to keep moving forward. Sometimes, things are kind of funny. James, at 8, attending a concert for my 7th grade niece was behaving appropriately (with pre-planned seating arrangements, and a piece of candy for after each song). The concert was the final one of the year, and awards were being given to the middle school students in the band. I looked at James to see if he was still doing ok, since there were no songs being played for a minute. He was in a grump, arms crossed, trying to kick the seat in front of him. He turned away from me and pouted when he saw me looking at him. I initially said "What happened? What didn't I see?" Then I realized that awards were being given, and half-joking said "You do know that the audience members don't get awards, right? Those are for the middle school band students. You are in second grade. In the audience." He looked at me, suddenly at ease, almost appearing pleased. I think he honestly likes to be called out on his feelings. Sometimes I'm not even sure he realizes what's upsetting him until it's thrown in his face. It was all I could do to keep from laughing out loud during the concert. I had been pleased as punch that my kids could attend an event like this, and trying not to let that overconfidence in their healing take over.

It's great to want them to be all better, but it's smart not to let yourself get tricked into believing that they are suddenly healed and normal. An 8 year old boy, smarter than most, pouting because he didn't get an award at a middle school band concert is funny. The best part about it is that he could see the humor in it, too. I teased him a little about it later, and he was able to join in. It was light-hearted, not mean, but I didn't really expect him to handle it. Someday I'll remind him of how he expected an award everywhere we went, but I doubt he'll believe me.

Sometimes, these reminders aren't so funny. Sometimes they are just sad. I can't bring my boys to visit my elderly friend at her care facility. The location is almost next door to their former grandmother's old house. They also think that every old lady looks like their former grandmother. Wherever we go, there are triggers. We might be at the store, at a social event (which is rare, but sometimes necessary), or just driving down the road. Any resemblance causes them anxiety, which often results in behavior problems. It's hard to go anywhere. Once, a lady came up to me in a store and asked if I knew where something was located. I responded, thinking nothing of it. She looked nothing like their former grandmother to me. The boys started acting inappropriately, which upset me immensely. We got out of there, and James told me that the lady looked like "Nana". Jackson agreed. I was so proud of them for sharing with me. It makes things so much easier to understand the behavior. I wasn't any less disturbed by their poor behavior throughout the day, but I reacted differently than if I had the belief that their behavior was not related to anxiety.

They did better that day than they could have, but it wasn't the easiest day ever. We'd planned to go to the zoo (not the "Nana" zoo), as kind of a birthday celebration for James. James was calling all of the animals "dummy heads" and shouting "You stupid things, go back there. Get away from me." He was labeling each thing we passed. "Green box... Big hat... Bear statue... Bird poop". It was great. He calmed down some, but was still somewhat difficult. He, did, at least, stop pulling all of the leaves off of the plants when I told him that they'd kick us out since it was a brand new exhibit. He also impressed the teen volunteer at the reptile building because he knew more than the guide. The teenager's friends (girls, maybe 15-16 years old) must have been impressed, too, as they texted a picture of my genius fact monster to someone. He is pretty amazing. Then there was Jackson. He had little to say, which is his way of dealing. He began to chase every animal that was not in an enclosure. I was worried the geese (near which there was a sign, warning of aggression due to nesting) were going to attack. Fortunately, or unfortunately, depending on how you look at it, the geese and Jackson were not harmed or intimidated. The duck, however, at our final exhibit, was not so fortunate. Upon leaving, this duck was waddling around in a semi-enclosed area in our exit path. The ape exhibit was on one side, with a plate glass window. A wall was on the other side, and above was open air and jungle-like plants, forming a tunnel. I was holding Jackson's hand, but he suddenly pulled away to chase that poor duck. I didn't expect what happened next, and I really wish it hadn't happened at all. It was a rather dreary day, with no sun. There must not have been any reflection on that window, and the duck flew forcefully into the glass with a loud "smack" and a muffled "honk". As if once wasn't enough, the poor confused duck with a head injury then attempted a second time. James laughed, but Jackson didn't. He may have wanted to scare the duck, but he didn't want to hurt one. The duck didn't try for the third time, thankfully, and just went waddling around instead. I hope the poor thing was all right, but honestly, we didn't stick around to find out. It was definitely time to go.

We are only just beginning to address the trauma in therapy. James has a really hard time with it. He has memories of violence and fighting, and is terrified of guns and knives. He has opened up about very little at this point. The trauma therapy has been difficult for me to witness, as he struggles with handling it. One thing that made it really hard from me was the way he tells the story. He's telling about things that happened many years ago- he must have been only a toddler at the time. When he tells about it, though- everything is in the present tense. He says things like "I go under the bed to hide when they start fighting". To me, it seemed like he would find it more appropriate to state it more like "I used to go under the bed to hide when they would fight." It was hard for me to understand, but when I asked the therapist about it, she explained that that's why the Post-Traumatic Stress Disorder diagnosis is relevant. He's still in the stressful state. He carries the trauma of the past with him, and will until it is addressed and accepted. She helped me to see why he spoke of these past events using the present tense, and why it's so important to deal with these problems. It just makes me sad he's lived his whole life in a state of fear. That must be a horrible way to be.

I am glad that we are moving through these issues, and that he has a chance for a happy life. I am deeply troubled by the idea that there are so many children that won't have that opportunity. It makes me want to help all of them, but I know that my sons need all of *me* to get better. It would be an injustice to them, as well as another child if I tried to take on anyone else with these kind of problems. I am happy with our family, even if it isn't what most would call "normal". We are going to be ok, and the road to happiness is within our reach. Here we are, nearing the end of our first two years together. We have been through so much, yet have so far to go. The hardest part is behind us, but the road ahead is long. I sometimes allow myself just a bit too much optimism, and try too hard to keep the boys moving forward. I have come to realize that regression, while difficult to accept, is a part of progress. Just recently, both of my sons were behaving remarkably well. They have developed skills for play that I didn't know they had. We were all seeming to be making great progress. They were happy, and I was happy. Although I wish that these moments of harmony were longer and permanent, I am grateful for the experience, however fleeting. I am seeing what we will have in the future. As quickly as the aggressive behaviors and opposition seemed to leave, it returned. I think that each child has a different reason for the struggle, too. For James, I think that addressing the trauma is difficult. He has a lot of memories that are becoming stirred up. I believe that he is ready to proceed and heal, but it's not easy. These things are hard to re-live, and he is forced to return to his familiar avoidance behaviors. It's not fun for either of us, but I know it's temporary. He's making progress. The behaviors have returned, but not with as much dominance. I had suspected that the behaviors were an indication that he was troubled, but I was sure when his pants were messy. It had been a really long time since the last time he'd done that. We talked about it, and I reassured him that it wasn't that big of a deal. The only thing he said was that he used to get in big trouble when he lived with "Papa". I reminded him that the messy pants just told me that I was right. We'd been talking about his behavior a lot lately, so it just meant that he was trying too hard not to think about something. I told him that it was just really nice that we didn't have messy pants every day anymore. It had been a really long time. The very next day, he tried really hard not to be avoidant and keep some control of his behavior while in my classroom (he happens to be in my school-age group right now). He had done much better than the few days before. He started getting upset as the evening progressed, but had sort of managed until he went to bring his bag in from the car. The string (that I had been telling him to cut off) had caught on the gate as he walked through. James lost it. He started crying his infantile cry- it's very much like an infant needing fed or changed. He opens his mouth wide, closes his eyes, and if you were hearing without seeing him, you'd think the sound was coming from a very young child. Anyway, I said- it's ok, just go get in the tub. He didn't move an inch. I said again, "I can tell you are very tired. You kept it together very well, but I think that you've met your limit. Go get in the tub." Still nothing. I went to get the bath ready, and go to retrieve him. What happened next, I never would have imagined. It was almost 2 years to the day since I'd had him. He had reverted back to some of his difficult behaviors over the last few days, after an amazing transformation into a happier, more "normal" child. He didn't dodge me when I approached, and I picked up my 8 year old son. I intended to carry him, stiffly as usual, to the bathroom and prod him along to get a bath. This time was different. He didn't pull away. For the first time ever, that child cuddled into my arms just like a newborn baby. He didn't have the stiff body, the unnatural position, the anger, fear, or silliness that had always accompanied such attempts at closeness. I stopped before we had reached the bathroom, and sat right on the floor, holding my son for the first time. We'd tried before, and had worked at being comfortable together. The closest he had come to being comfortable was while we watched something on TV or a movie on the couch. Sometimes while reading a story, he would relax enough to "feel" comfortable. This was the first time that he allowed me to comfort him. I listened as his cries very quickly faded, and we just sat. This was it? The fit that I expected to last through the bath and until I physically placed him in bed- it was over? I told him that I had noticed how hard he had worked to keep things together all day long. I let him know how proud I was that he had done that. I said that it must have taken so much strength to do that all day long. His body just couldn't do it anymore. He'd done a great job all day, but it was time to let it all out.

I just could not believe that he allowed me to be there to help him through it. After having a few difficult days, his apparent comfort with me was the last thing I ever could have imagined would happen. If you have never participated in an attempt to comfort a child that cannot be comforted, the concept is likely unbelievable. I, however, had been jabbed, kicked, pinched, poked, licked, bitten, wrestled, bounced upon, pushed, pulled, grabbed, and prodded through countless attempts to sit comfortably with my sons. Jackson came around first, but still would not fall asleep while sitting on or near me for a year and a half. Jackson didn't do as much poking and wiggling, but avoided the contact for a while.

James had a different way of interacting with touch. He would seek it, but only in inappropriate ways. Everything had been forced, and his body was more like a weapon. He would use so much pressure with any kind of hug, hand holding, and even sitting was unpleasant. I didn't realize that anyone could sit "hard", but James could. Even when the time came that he did learn how to "melt" into my arms, he still couldn't sit at a movie theater and touch me. He wanted to lie on me, but he would use so much pressure with his head that my circulation would be cut off. I would wait until I could stand it no more, so as to prolong the closeness. My hand would be cold to the touch and aching, but I held on as long as I could. He would sit on my lap, but it was not even close to being comfortable- for me or for him. It was like he had stony points being rolled over every part of my body. It seemed like he knew every tender spot and could put pressure on it with extreme precision. I know he really didn't have the conscious intention to do so, but the act of sitting with him was painful and exhausting. The sitting while watching a movie at home on the couch, and while reading some books was nice. I didn't know that he could ever manage to allow himself to be comfortable in my arms, especially after being upset. This was a whole new concept. I feel a bit odd about being so moved by this one interaction, but that's just the way it is. My 8 year old son had finally managed to accept me as a caregiver. He allowed me to comfort him. He may have acted like a toddler, but he acted like a toddler. We were moving beyond newborn and into toddlerhood. He had maintained some posture- sitting up. He had not been lying down drooling or staring off into space. He did sound like a baby, but it didn't last all night. I had held my son for the first time. I didn't care that he was nearly 60 pounds. I didn't care that he was 8 years old. I cared that he had sought comfort in me. This was a big deal. A very big deal.

Jackson had me puzzled. I knew his friend from his class moved away, and that when summer came, I could no longer pick him up in the afternoons as I had been. I thought that maybe those might have been reasons for him to be more agitated. He's also got to be very tired. The summer schedule is grueling. One particularly rough day (he even acted out a little in front of others), I talked to him about it. He had wanted to watch a video, but I'd already let him play a video game, and typically weekdays do not allow for tablet time. I had said no, and gave a few reasons, including the fact that we don't usually do that on weekdays, and reminded him that his behavior wasn't exactly so hot that day. Then he had gone into the "I'm just bad" mode.

I was trying to help him figure out what was going on that gave him such trouble lately. I mentioned the friend moving, the afternoons spent at daycare, and a few other ideas. Then I finally came right out and said "This is about the same time of year that I got you. Are you worried about me leaving you? Do you think that something might change?" I didn't expect the response I got. I really didn't. He was on the floor, on his back, and had been shaking his head "no" for all of my other suggestions. This time, his face turned into a frown, and before he rolled over to hide his face, he nodded his head. I couldn't believe it. Had I really guessed it? Then it all made sense. He had been doing so well. He had been my little sweetheart, recently. He'd been affectionate and kind, loving and calm. The last week or two had been... *hard*. The "pushing away" behaviors were back. He refused to hold my hand when I walked with him. The racing between James and him had begun again. The "I hate you face" had returned. Things had been thrown at me. He'd said hurtful things like "I don't have a mom," "You only love James, not me," and "I just don't want you anymore". Of course! He had become worried about me leaving him. He had to create the chaos again. He wanted to make me reject him.

I felt incredibly hurt that my son thought that I'd ever leave him. I felt angry that my poor baby had been hurt in such a way that he developed those thoughts. I felt relieved that I could finally understand the language of my children. I didn't have to go through life misunderstanding what they were telling me anymore (at least not quite as much). The behaviors are just as difficult, but having a more appropriate perception changes everything. I see the hurt child, rather than the hurtful one. It isn't easy, and I still don't always do the right thing, but we are together in our struggle. What really amazed me was his admission of the concept. I didn't expect him to agree, even if that was really going on in his head. I was a bit worried to be putting some thoughts in his head that might not have been there otherwise. The way he reacted confirmed my suspicions, and thankfully didn't seem to cause him additional stress from irrelevant ideas. He did much better the following night, too.

I still have a hard time when I realize how much stress these boys carry with them all of the time. Jackson internalizes more, too, so it takes me a while to catch on. I don't know if he can actually sense the time of year, or if there are certain objects that trigger these thoughts. I know that the boys have discussed the fireworks tents as they are put up. The 4th of July weekend was the first time they stayed with me, and I would get them for good about 2 weeks later. Those fireworks stands might offer more of a concrete trigger, I'm not sure. What I do know, is that there is no way for anyone else to pick up on these behaviors. No one else sees them as any different when they are going through a rough time. I have learned to keep my thoughts to myself, because sharing my observations is risky. Most people only see the surface, and do not see anything different in my kids at all during these times. I have doubted myself on many occasions, but when my suspicions are validated- usually by something like soiled pants- I can be confident that I know my kids. I recognize that the violent fits and demands for more hugs, while obvious attempts at control, have a greater purpose. My children struggle to develop and maintain a feeling of trust, security, and safety. The little behavior quirks and facial expressions are subtle, but I now see through them, and realize that something has gotten my children upset. No one else may see it, or might see the behaviors as just naughtiness. Their perception doesn't mean that it isn't really happening. My recognition of the behaviors doesn't necessarily mean that I completely understand them, either. I just have better insight into the hurt they are suffering, and can cope better with the problems that arise.

The behaviors, while difficult, are simply the language of my children. They don't speak the same language as most children, and can be understood by only a select few. There are so many things that our family looks upon with a different view. Even things that no one else would think twice about have created memorable experiences. Not very long ago, during a feelings game in therapy, Jackson needed to come up with something that makes me feel sad. He was pretty tired, and not so cooperative that day, but the therapist was giving him a bit of a boost to help him out. She gave him some ideas that were supposed to be off the wall. She said "Bubble gum- does that make Mom sad?" He and I caught each other's eyes, and laughed, as we knew that bubble gum really does have potential to make me distressed. I've taken it away "until the next birthday", but finally settled on "a long time from now", since right after each of their birthdays we still had trouble with bubble gum. Neither of them can keep it in their mouths! Jackson takes it out and plays with it, James ends up with it all over his face and anything around him. It is always a disaster! I am not talking about 2 or 3 year old children, here. They are now 5 and 8 and still cannot handle chewing bubble gum. The therapist was surprised to find out that she had indeed given Jackson more of a hint than she intended. It was OK, though. Even bubble gum can cause major stress in a family like ours.

I can tell you, without any doubt, that the last two years have been rough. We have struggled. I have struggled. Without the incredible support from my family, our therapist, and our support group, I don't know where we'd be right now. I don't want to give the impression that I think we are done healing, because we aren't. Even as I end this story with an incredible sense of optimism, reality is present. Last week, the "I hate you face" from Jackson returned, and James had a fit tonight that was very close to the "dying cow" fits of the past. Things are good, though, better than they've ever been. I am stronger, and my sons are growing into who they really are. There are scars that will never disappear, but the pain is beginning to fade. The boys have a chance now, and with that, our family does, too. I am more in debt than I'd care to think about, the house is a mess, and I constantly stress about being able to provide for my children in the way they deserve. However, things are working out. My parents are supportive, and thankfully, have been helpful with loans. The house is getting closer to being our home, even if the boys are still scared here. Things will get better. I know it. They already have.

When I began writing our story, I was feeling such elation with our family's success. I still have that feeling, even as some of the boys' behaviors returned before I was done looking over what I'd written, and decided to include the difficulties we were dealing with. The regressions, while still difficult, are bearable now. I don't enjoy being kicked, climbed on, or have things thrown at me. I don't like to watch James climb on the furniture during therapy, while only remaining somewhat still during the time he's biting his toenails (Ewww!). I am saddened when Jackson has to test the limits again, just to know I'm still here. I try to take on the pain as they work through their trauma, but I can only be here to comfort them. It doesn't feel like enough, but it's more than I could do before. I admit, however, that their return of behaviors gave me insight and reminders of our past, which comes with a great sense of appreciation. This is only a tiny taste of what our past once was. Even through the difficulties we are still encountering, nothing can compare to what our family was not so long ago.

As I worked on writing our story, I debated sharing it with others. I'm ashamed of some of the things I did, and I spent so much time confused about what was really going on- it's embarrassing. As I wrote, I discovered that it was very therapeutic. The goal of telling our story is to help others feel as if they aren't alone. If someone reads our story and can relate to the type of experiences we endured, then it has been worth it. I may continue writing, as our story is not yet over. For now, though, please know that I am blessed with what I have been given. I don't know if all families can be successful after adopting children with RAD and PTSD. I know that there are children with behavior challenges that are beyond what can be dealt with in the home. I do not have all the answers, and won't pretend I do. I also won't pretend that I could have made it through those tough times without the unfaltering support of my parents, and our therapist. I am scared to think too much about where we would be without our devoted therapist. She pulled us out of our misery, and is pushing us through as we emerge as a family. She, undoubtedly, is a part of that family. Perspective is what I needed, and without her knowledge and extraordinary ability to truly understand these kids and parents like me, I'd still be looking from the outside in. I continue to make mistakes, but things are so much better now, since I have a better understanding of who my children are, and who I am. Together, we make a family, and no matter how others perceive us, we are now becoming "just fine".

Never a Dull Moment

Some memories I have didn't seem to have a place in our story, or I can't quite recall exactly when it happened. There are a few additional thoughts, humorous incidents, and confessions that I think are relevant, too. I've included them here:

One morning, I spoke to James after he brushed his teeth and made a mess, telling him to make sure that next time he spit his toothpaste into the sink, not all over it. Jackson went to brush his teeth right after, and when I went to turn the light off, I saw that not one inch had been missed. Jackson had sprayed everything with toothpaste spit. The sink, counter, and faucet were all spattered, just to prove that he might just be the most defiant child alive.

James shared with me about a boy at school that knew lots of facts. The way James described the knowledge the other child had, it seemed to me that he might have an obsession with certain facts, as some children, like those with autism sometimes do. I asked James "Is this boy 'special', a little different than most kids?" James, without missing a beat, said "No, he lives with his birthmother."

233

I had to tell the therapist once about an argument I had with my sister. It involved yelling, which upset the boys, and I had been very angry. I'm pretty sure I slammed the door, too. I hung my head and confessed to her, trying to explain why the kids were likely triggered. Instead of feeling put-down, she simply asked whether the argument had been over an issue concerning the boys. It had. She said very matter-of-factly that it happens, and the arguments are usually over something involving the kids. I can't begin to describe how relieved I was to have that burden of guilt lifted. I knew it wasn't good that I had behaved that way, but it helped to know that it was common and not completely detrimental to the future well-being of my boys.

I was (and still am) overly cautious about monitoring the boys while they play, especially in the yard. They could somehow make a simple activity like playing outside turn into a terrible, yet memorable experience. There have been swings broken, rocks thrown, ropes used for everything except jumping, flowers picked, squash smashed, bubbles mixed with ants, and many other activities. Many people might agree that all kids might do things like that. I do, too, to a point. I might be the only parent, however, that has had to say these words: "What is that? Put that dead squirrel DOWN!" I once looked out the kitchen window to see Jackson holding a dead squirrel up in the air by the tail. I was less than pleased.

There were (and are) many times when my children are absolutely impossible to please. Jackson has an extreme dedication to the idea of being impossible. He would decide that anything was wrong, even if he'd asked for it. In the car sometimes, he would decide that he was either "too hot" or "too cold". I initially fell into the trap, believing that there was indeed a possibility that this child could be made more comfortable by adjusting the temperature. I would turn up the heat or air conditioning, but sometimes gave the expected response of "You're fine!" which was what was desired. That way an argument could ensue. A few times, with no real thought process going on, I responded to Jackson's requests with extreme temperature adjustments. Poor James never complained, but I feel bad subjecting him, too, to the uncomfortable temperature. Jackson never admitted that he was uncomfortable when I responded to his cries of displeasure by turning up the control to "high". He did, however, in a way, admit that it was all a game. Instead of continuing on with the "I'm hot, I'm hot" or "I'm cold, I'm cold", he went to a new chant that alternated each statement of discontent: "I'm hot, I'm cold. I'm hot, I'm cold". There is no winning.

James, a very picky eater at first, surprised me by trying fried rice at a restaurant once. I had requested an order of rice, intending to share a little, but expecting James to eat more of the chicken nuggets and potato smiles that was part of the kid's meal I'd ordered for both boys. James not only tried the fried rice, but gave the impression that he was starved and attempted to eat all of it. He was rather ill-looking the rest of the day. He actually admitted that he tried to eat it all so I couldn't have any. Parents of "normal" kids might think that it's funny- once. For those of you who live with a child like James, I am willing to bet that you understand that it really does feel like your own child is "out to get you" on a daily basis. It ceases to be funny.

When the boys first came, I expected that Jackson would be the "baby". Although we'd later discover that he had severe problems, James was the child that seemed to show more signs of abnormality. When he came to me at 6 years old, he did not know how to blow his nose or wipe after toileting (assuming that I did manage to get him to use the bathroom appropriately). I had to hold the tissue to his nose and give instructions to "blow". I found this very hard to deal with. I didn't think that a 6 year old child would need to be taught these basic life skills.

Both boys loved to hear stories right from the start. Jackson was especially enthralled with any book. Even when I read chapter books, Jackson could relate a character to someone he knew. I was impressed. One book I read within the first 6 months of being together was extremely meaningful to him. It had very few words, but seemed to tell a big story in Jackson's mind. In the story, a little bunny and mother are shown, and they become separated (the little bunny leaves because he's mad). The mother rabbit sits up and looks for her bunny, and the bunny returns. It didn't seem that significant to me. Jackson cried. He cried real tears, and asked me to read it again. He wanted that book again, and again, and again. He cried every time. One day, he said "I don't want to read that book again," and that was that. I'm still not sure whether the part that he relates to most is when the bunny leaves, or if it is when the bunny returns and the mother and child are reunited. Regardless, I was intrigued by the fact that a 3 year old could be moved to tears by a book. It was interesting and sad. Someday I'll read it again to him, and see what happens.

My attempts to heal the boys were often misguided and downright foolish. Our therapist gave us "homework" to support healing at home. Relaxation techniques were to be practiced, along with time set aside for each child. I tried to set it up so each child could watch an episode of some show during the other child's time with me. I was scheduling relaxation. It sounds odd, but similarly to the incident described earlier involving me trying to force relaxation, it was a complete failure. I found myself saying through clenched teeth, "Hurry up and RELAX!" This was not working. We finally managed to set things up better, but it took quite a while for me to catch on.

A recent discussion at the breakfast table concluded that we all look forward to Fridays- therapy days. James said that he liked therapy days because he gets to play his tablet for a long time. I said that there might be better reasons to like Fridays. Jackson, with a smug little grin, said "I like Fridays because I know that therapy will make our hearts healthy." He is a funny little guy.

At the beginning of this year, I got a wall calendar for both boys. I write something positive on each one every day. I realized, at first, that many of my positives were negatives in disguise. The ability to "not" do something is actually quite commendable when referring to my boys. Some examples of our "calendar worthy" accomplishments:

You only had a little fit when you found out you had to get a haircut.
You drained the water in the bathtub.
You didn't get me all wet when I got you out of the tub.
You cleaned up the pee in the bathroom without a fit.
You handled it when you saw what we were having for supper.
You did great when we had to wait for our food at the restaurant.
You didn't have a big fit when the battery died.
You were quiet while I was on the phone.
You didn't have a fit when I asked you to pick up your clothes.
You picked up your clothes when I asked you to.
You called me "Mama".
You helped your brother try to buckle.
You put the sucker stick in the trash.
You asked for a bedtime kiss.
You tried refried beans at supper, and didn't have a fit.
You came to me when you were scared.
You sat with me when we watched the movie.
You wiped your face before wiping it on my shirt.

237

You didn't have a fit when we had to pause the show.
You didn't have a big fit when you thought your toy was lost.
You recovered from your big fit and had a good evening.
You picked up your pajamas, and your brother's too.
You didn't have a fit when you had to clean your pants out.
You told the truth about giving your friend your vitamins.
You stayed in the yard.
You talked with me WITH eye contact.
You played alone for almost 15 minutes!
You thanked your aunt for the book she gave you.
You apologized twice today and made good choices.
You said you liked sitting with me.
You did great at Walmart.
You didn't have a fit when you realized it wasn't a therapy day.
You tried hard to work on eye contact.
You told me how you were feeling.
You left Grandma's house without a fit.
You told me about your day at school.
You didn't interrupt when it was your brother's turn.
You let me help you feel better.
You sat nicely with me for a little while.
You handled not getting candy.
You read your lunchbox note.
You did well even when we had other people around.
You said "I love my house".
You were doing what you were supposed to be doing twice!
You got over having to go to the store.
You did great when you had to handle not getting McDonalds.
You handled things really well when our plans changed.
You didn't have a fit when it was time to go to bed.
You had so much fun playing today.

If you are a parent of a difficult child, these statements probably aren't at all silly. If you don't view "You cleaned up your pee without a fit" as an accomplishment, then you haven't experienced life the way we do. In one way, it's sad that these things are noteworthy, but in another, it's a blessing to be able to celebrate these small things. There are many great things to come for us, but the small things are worth noticing, now. They really aren't small, either. It's the perception. When recalling those car trips with shrill screams, the peaceful drives with pleasant conversation are that much more appreciated. When every meal was more like a circus, one time sitting and talking nicely, while eating, is an incredible experience. When you've gone almost 2 years without ever seeing your children actually play together, 5 minutes of play is an incredible sight. After constantly seeing only hurt, anger; sadness, and vengefulness, the moment you witness real joy and hear laughter is indescribable. I think that these small victories are truly worth celebrating.

As I continue to learn, and work to help my children heal, I notice more about the way life is. We are never going to be like other families, but we're becoming a happy one. People wonder if I regret the choice I made to adopt my sons. I do not. I regret some of the things I did along the way, and would have prepared myself differently if I knew then what I know now. I would have prepared for my own hurt feelings much better, and been a little bit "harder". I would have been just as helpful to my kids, but tried to avoid letting their attempts to hurt me become successful. I would have started out with a much bigger loan. I would have started out with more structure, and more confidence in my own thoughts. I would have trusted my own instincts, rather than taking the input from everyone else. I would have started therapy sooner. I feel very grateful that we are fortunate enough to have an experienced, knowledgeable therapist. I feel confident that my children will be healed. I don't think that all families are as fortunate, and I cannot begin to imagine the heartbreak of having to accept failure after putting everything you have into healing your child.

Please know that I do not have all of the answers, and that the struggle for us is not yet over. I honestly believe that we have progressed through the most challenging part of the healing process, but know that we have a very long way to go. If you are reading this, and are still going through that really hard time, I can tell you that for us, things did get better. Finding our therapist is what saved us. I don't like to think of where we'd be without her. Having my mom to support me is also a big thing. She actually understands. My dad is beginning to see the truth, too. He saw the boys before, and recognizes the difference. It took longer, though, as it seemed to him that I was the one making things difficult. My sister and brother are not terrible, but they don't see my children as being any different than their children. My boys have invisible scars; hidden wounds that are revealed only to a select few. My sister, just recently, was teasing my boys about "trading" a little boy for a big one- her 17 year old (they'd been having a big argument that day). James, of course, was practically in her car ready to go, but Jackson- he actually looked frightened. I am ashamed to admit that I was pleased at my son's discomfort. He wanted me. He really did. If you are a parent who understands these issues, and aren't able to feel that yet, I pray that you get the chance. I waited a very long time, but it was worth it. Some of us are lucky enough to taste that sweetness- when the fruit begins to ripen.

www.ingramcontent.com/pod-product-compliance
Lightning Source LLC
LaVergne TN
LVHW051045080426
835508LV00019B/1706